KAREN BROWN'S

English

Country Bed & Breakfasts

KAREN BROWN TITLES

California Country Inns & Itineraries

English Country Bed & Breakfasts

English, Welsh & Scottish Country Hotels & Itineraries

French Country Bed & Breakfasts

French Country Inns & Itineraries

German Country Inns & Itineraries

Irish Country Inns & Itineraries

Italian Country Bed & Breakfasts

Italian Country Inns & Itineraries

Spanish Country Inns & Itineraries

Swiss Country Inns & Itineraries

KAREN BROWN'S

English
Country Bed & Breakfasts

Written by

JUNE BROWN

Sketches by Barbara Tapp

Cover Painting by Jann Pollard

Travel Press

Karen Brown's Country Inn Series

Travel Press editors: Iris Sandilands, Karen Brown, Clare Brown, Susanne Lau Alloway
Technical support: William H. Brown III; Aide-de-camp: William H. Brown
Illustrations: Barbara Tapp; Cover painting: Jann Pollard
Maps: Susanne Lau Alloway—Greenleaf Design & Graphics

Distributed USA & Canada: The Globe Pequot Press, tel: (203)395-0440, fax: (203) 395-0312
Box 833, Old Saybrook, CT 06475
Distributed Europe: Springfield Books Ltd., tel: (01484) 864 955, fax: (01484) 865 443
Norman Road., Denby Dale, Huddersfield HD8 8TH, W. Yorkshire, England,
A catalog record for this book is available from the British Library
Distributed Australia: Little Hills Press Pty. Ltd., tel: (02) 437-6995, fax: (02) 438-5762
1st Floor, Regent House, 37-43 Alexander St, Crows Nest NSW 2065, Australia
Distributed New Zealand: Tandem Press Ltd., tel: (0064) 9 480-1452, fax: (0064) 9 480 1455
P.O. Box 34-272, Birkenhead, Auckland 10, New Zealand

Library of Congress Cataloging-in-Publication Data
Brown, June, 1949-
    Karen Brown's English country bed & breakfasts / written by June
Brown.
        p. cm. -- (Karen Brown's country inn series)
    Includes index.
    ISBN 0-930328-29-9 : $15.95
    1. Bed and breakfast accommodations--England--Guidebooks.
2. England--Guidebooks. I. Brown, Karen. II. Title: III. Title:
 English country bed and breakfasts. IV. Series.
TX907.5.G72.E5433 1994
647.944203--dc20
                                              92-113777
                                               CIP

Dedicated With Love And Thanks
To My Parents
Gladys and George

Contents

Introduction

Castleton

English Country Bed & Breakfasts describes accommodations that are special. They vary from a romantic thatched cottage down a leafy lane to a grand ancestral manor. Interspersed with these lovely homes are traditional pubs and guesthouses that offer wholehearted hospitality in charming surroundings. Every place to stay is one that we have seen and enjoyed—our personal recommendation. We sincerely believe that where you lay your head each night makes the difference between a good and a great vacation. We encourage you to buy the new editions of our guides and throw away old ones—you will be glad you did. With every revision we delete places that have not maintained our standards, add many enchanting new bed and breakfasts, and update prices, phone, and fax numbers. Your comments and suggestions are invaluable. Please write. Thank you.

Karen Brown's Guides, P.O. Box 70, San Mateo CA 94401, USA

About Bed And Breakfast Travel

Every place to stay in this book has a different approach to bed-and-breakfast. Some households are very informal, some welcome children, and others invite you to sample gracious living, cocktails in the drawing room, billiards after dinner, and croquet on the lawn. The one thing that they have in common is a warmth of welcome. We have tried to be candid and honest in our appraisals and tried to convey each listing's special flavor so that you know what to expect and will not be disappointed. **None of the places to stay ever pays to be included.** To help you appreciate and understand what to expect when staying at places in this guide the following pointers are given in alphabetical order, not order of importance.

ANIMALS

Even if animals are not mentioned in the write-up, the chances are that there are friendly, tail-wagging dogs and sleek cats as visible members of the families.

ARRIVAL AND DEPARTURE

Always discuss your time of arrival—hosts usually expect you to arrive around 6:00 pm. If you are going to arrive late or early, be certain to telephone your host. You are expected to leave by 10:00 am on the morning of your departure. By and large you are not expected to be on the premises during the day.

BATHROOMS

Stating that a bedroom has a private bathroom indicates that the bathroom is for the exclusive use of one bedroom, but it may be down the hall or ensuite in the room.

BEDROOMS

Beds are often made with duvets (down comforters) instead of the more traditional blankets and sheets. A double room has one double bed, a twin room has two single beds, and a family room contains one or more single beds in addition to a double bed. American king and queen beds are few and far between.

CHILDREN

Places that welcome children state "Children welcome." The majority of listings in this guide do not "welcome" children but find they become tolerable at different ages over 5 or, more often than not, over 12. In some cases places simply do not accept children and the listing states "Children not accepted." However, these indications of children's acceptability are not cast in stone, so if you have your heart set on staying at a listing that accepts children over 12 and you have an 8-year-old, call them, explain your situation, and they may well take you. Ideally we would like to see all listings welcoming children and all parents remembering that they are staying in a home and doing their bit by making sure that children do not run wild. A list of places that "welcome" children of any age is given at the back of this book.

CHRISTMAS

Several listings offer Christmas getaways. If the information section indicates that the listing is open during the Christmas season, there is a very good chance that it offers a festive Christmas package.

CREDIT CARDS

The majority of places in this guide do not accept plastic payment. If the accommodation accepts payment by credit card it is indicated using the terms AX, American Express, EC, Eurocard, MC, Master Card, VS, Visa, or simply all major.

DIRECTIONS

We give concise driving directions to guide you to the listing which is often in a more out-of-the-way place than the town or village in the address. We would be very grateful if you would let us know of cases where our directions have proved inadequate.

ELECTRICITY

The voltage is 240. Most bathrooms have razor points (American style) for 110 volts. If you are coming from overseas it is recommended that you take only dual voltage appliances and a kit of electrical plugs. Often your host can loan you a hairdryer and an iron.

Rye

Introduction—About Bed and Breakfast Travel

MAPS

Each Place to Stay is referenced to one of the maps at the back of this guide showing the location of the town or village nearest the lodging. These artist's renderings are not intended to replace commercial maps. Our suggestion is to purchase a large-scale road atlas of England where an inch equals 10 miles. Our maps can be cross referenced with those in our companion guide *English, Welsh & Scottish Country Hotels & Itineraries* which has the added attraction of countryside driving itineraries.

MEALS

Prices quoted always include breakfast. Breakfast is most likely to be juice, a choice of porridge or cereal, followed by a plate of egg, bacon, sausage, tomatoes, and mushrooms completed by toast, marmalade, and jams. A great many places offer evening meals which should be requested at the time you make your reservation. You cannot expect to arrive at a bed-and-breakfast and receive dinner if you have not made reservations for it several days in advance. At some homes the social occasion of guests and host gathered around the dining-room table for an evening dinner party is a large part of the overall experience and many of these types of listings expect their guests to dine in. Places that do not offer evening meals are always happy to make recommendations for guests at nearby pubs or restaurants.

RATES

Rates are those quoted to us for the 1995 summer season. We have tried to standardize rates by quoting the 1995 per person bed-and-breakfast rate based on two people occupying a room. Not all places conform, so where dinner is included or the listing only quotes the double rate we have stated this in the listing. Prices are always quoted to include breakfast, Value Added Tax (VAT), and service (if these are applicable). Please use the figures printed as a guideline and be certain to ask what the rate is at the time of booking. Prices for a single are usually higher than the per-person rates and prices for a family room are sometimes lower. Many listings offer special terms, below their normal prices, for "short breaks" of two or more nights. In several listings suites are available at higher prices.

RESERVATIONS

Reservations can be confining and usually must be guaranteed by a deposit; however, if you have your heart set on a particular place, to avoid disappointment make a reservation. If you prefer to travel as whim and the weather dictate, rooms can often be had in the countryside with just a few days' notice. July and August are the busiest times and if you are traveling to a popular spot such as Bath or York it is advisable to make reservations. It is completely unacceptable practice to make reservations for a particular night at several establishments, choosing at the last minute which one to stay at.

Although proprietors do not always strictly adhere to it, it is important to understand that once reservations are confirmed whether by phone or in writing you are under contract. This means that the proprietor is legally obligated to provide the accommodation he has promised and that you are bound to pay for that accommodation. If you cannot take up your accommodation, you are liable for a portion of the accommodation charges plus your deposit. If you have to cancel your reservation, do so as soon as possible so that the proprietor can attempt to re-let your room in which case you are liable only for the re-let fee or the deposit.

If you are visiting from overseas, our preference for making a reservation is by telephone; the cost is minimal and you have your answer immediately, so if space is not available you can then decide on an alternate. (If calling from the United States allow for the time difference [England is five hours ahead of New York] so that you can call during their business day. Dial 011 [the international code], 44 [Britain's code], then the city code (dropping the 0), and the telephone number.) Be specific as to what your needs are, such as a ground-floor room, ensuite bathroom or twin beds. Check the prices which may well have changed from those given in the book (summer 1995). Ask what deposit to send or give your credit card number. Tell them about what time you intend to arrive and request dinner if you want it. Ask for a confirmation letter with brochure and map to be sent to you.

Shaftesbury

SIGHTSEEING

We have tried to mention major sightseeing attractions near each lodging to encourage you to spend several nights in each location. Few countries have as much to offer as England. Within a few miles of every listing there are places of interest to visit and explore: lofty cathedrals, quaint churches, museums, and grand country houses. Our companion guide *English, Welsh & Scottish Country Hotels & Itineraries* includes countryside driving itineraries that are useful in helping you plan your holiday.

SMOKING

Nearly all listings forbid smoking either in the bedrooms or public rooms. Some allow no smoking at all, in which case we state "No Smoking house." A list of no smoking houses is at the back of the book. Ask about smoking policies if this is important to you—best to be forewarned rather than frustrated.

Polperro

SOCIALIZING

We have tried to indicate the degree of socializing that is included in your stay as some hosts treat their guests like visiting friends and relatives, sharing cocktails, eating with them around the dining room table, and joining them for coffee after dinner (the difference being that friends and relatives do not receive a bill at the end of their stay).

WOLSEY LODGES

Several of the listings are members of Wolsey Lodges, a consortium of private houses that open their doors to a handful of guests at a time. Visitors become a part of the household, guests are not expected to scuttle up to their rooms and family life does not carry on away from guests behind closed doors. Everyone usually dines together round a polished table, and unless you make special requests, you eat what is served to you. The conversation flows and you meet those you might never have met elsewhere. Early or late in the season you may find that you are the only guests in these houses and you can enjoy a romantic candlelit dinner in a house full of character and charm. You are welcome as guests because you are the ones who help the owners pay their central heating bills, private school fees, and gardeners. As with all the listings in this guide, Wolsey Lodge members approach bed-and-breakfast in different ways—some are informal, while others offer a taste of refined, gracious living. If a lodging is a member of this group, we state "Wolsey Lodge" in the information section. A brochure listing all the Wolsey Lodge properties is available from Wolsey Lodges, 17 Chapel Street, Bildeston, Suffolk IP7 7EP, tel: 01449 741297, fax: 01449 741590. Places in this guide that are members of Wolsey Lodges are listed at the back of the book.

About England

DRIVING

Just about the time overseas visitors board their return flight home they will have adjusted to driving on the "right" side which is the left side in England. You must contend with such things as roundabouts (circular intersections); flyovers (overpasses); ring roads (peripheral roads whose purpose is to bypass city traffic); lorries (trucks); lay bys (turn outs); boots (trunks), and bonnets (hoods). Pedestrians are permitted to cross the road anywhere and always have the right of way. Seat belts must be worn at all times

Motorways: The letter "M" precedes these convenient ways to cover long distances. With three lanes of traffic either side of a central divider, you should stay in the left-hand lane except for passing. Motorway exits are numbered and correspond to numbering on major road maps. Service areas supply petrol, cafeterias, and "bathrooms" (the word "bathroom" is used in the American sense—in Britain "bathroom" means a room with a shower or bathtub, not a toilet: "loo" is the most commonly used term for an American bathroom).

"A" Roads: The letter "A" precedes the road number. All major roads fall into this category. They vary from three lanes either side of a dividing barrier to single carriageways with an unbroken white line in the middle indicating that passing is not permitted. These roads have the rather alarming habit of changing from dual to single carriageway.

"B" Roads and Country Roads: The letter "B" preceding the road number or the lack of any lettering or numbering indicate that it belongs to the maze of country roads that crisscross Britain. These are the roads for people who have the luxury of time to enjoy the scenery en route. Arm yourself with a good map (although getting lost is part of the fun). Driving these narrow roads is terrifying at first but exhilarating after a while. Meandering down these roads, you can expect to spend time crawling behind a tractor or cows being herded to the farmyard. Some lanes are so narrow that there is room for only one car.

INFORMATION

The British Tourist Authority (BTA) is an invaluable source of information. Their major offices are located as follows:

AUSTRALIA–SYDNEY
BTA, 8th Floor, 210 Clarence Street, Sydney, NSW 2000, tel: 02 267 4555

CANADA–TORONTO
BTA, 111 Avenue Road, Suite 450, Toronto, Ontario M5R 3J8, tel: (416) 961 8124

FRANCE–PARIS
BTA, Maison de la Grand Bretagne, 19 rue des Mathurins, 75009 Paris, tel: 1 4451 5620

GERMANY–FRANKFURT
BTA, Taunusstrasse 52-6-60329 Frankfurt 1, tel: 069 2380711

USA–NEW YORK
BTA, 551 Fifth Ave., New York NY 10176, tel: 800 462 2748, or in NY tel: (212) 986 2200

If you need additional information while you are in Britain, there are more than 700 official Tourist Information Centres identified by a blue and white letter "i" and "Tourist Information."

In London the British Travel Centre at 12 Regent Street, London SW1 (near Piccadilly Circus tube station) provides information on what to see and do, and how to do it, all year round in Britain. There are an American Express travel service office, a bureau de change, and a British Rail ticket office there, so you can book a room, buy air or train tickets, hire a car, or pay for a coach tour or theater tickets in one location. The Centre also has changing exhibitions put on by the National and Regional Tourist Boards, and a "video wall" where several screens display films of attractions to be found round the country. The Centre is open seven days a week, 9:00 am to 6:30 pm Monday to Saturday, 10:00 am to 4:00 pm on Sunday.

PUBS

Pubs are a British institution. Traditional pubs with inviting names such as the Red Lion, Wheatsheaf, and Kings Arms are found at the heart of every village. Not only are they a great place to meet the locals over a pint or a game of dominoes or darts, but they offer an inviting place to dine. Food served in the bar enables you to enjoy an inexpensive meal while sipping your drink in convivial surroundings. Bar meals range from a bowl of soup to a delicious cooked dinner. Many pubs have dining rooms that serve more elaborate fare in equally convivial but more sophisticated surroundings. The key to success when dining at a pub is to obtain a recommendation from where you are staying that night—your host is always happy to assist you.

Kersey

Introduction—About England

SHOPPING

Overseas visitors can reclaim the VAT (Value Added Tax) paid on the goods they purchase. Not all stores participate in the refund scheme and there is often a minimum purchase price. Stores that do participate will ask to see your passport before completing the VAT form. This form must be presented with the goods to the Customs officer at the point of departure from Britain within three months of purchase. The customs officer will certify the form which you return to the store where you bought the goods. The store will then send you a check in sterling for the refund.

WEATHER

Britain has a tendency to be moist at all times of the year. The cold in winter is rarely severe; however, the farther north you go the greater the possibility of being snowed in. Spring can be wet, but it is a lovely time to travel; the summer crowds have not descended, daffodils and bluebells fill the woodlands, and the hedgerows are filled with wildflowers. Summer offers the best chance of sunshine, but also the largest crowds. Schools are usually closed the last two weeks of July and all of August so this is the time when most families take their summer holidays. Travel is especially hectic on the weekends in summer—try to avoid major routes and airports at these times. Autumn is also an ideal touring time. The weather tends to be drier than in spring and the woodlands are decked in their golden autumn finery.

Lower Slaughter

Places to Stay

We found Judith and David Pritchard busy in the garden and kitchen picking blackcurrants and redcurrants and cooking them into jams and jellies. As we accompanied them through their fruit and vegetable garden we realized why they have no time for the swimming pool, the sauna or the tennis court—the garden and the care of their guests is a full-time occupation. The Pritchards' easy, friendly manner soon has you feeling at home. While guests are welcome to use the large, formal drawing room they often prefer to sit cozily by the fire in the hall parlor. Judith is happy to prepare dinner, and guests are usually served at separate tables. Upstairs the most spacious bedroom is Mogul (named for the Indian prints that hang upon the flowery wallpaper) which has a full bathroom and a separate shower. In addition there are two double bedrooms and a small single room that can accommodate a child. Fly fishing folk enjoy fishing the nearby Rivers Test, Avon, and Itchen. Salisbury and Winchester are within easy reach as is Broadlands (Mountbatten's home at Romsey) and Highclere Castle with its Egyptian treasures. *Directions:* From the A303 (near Andover) take the A343, Salisbury road, and take the first right turn down a very narrow, unmarked lane: Abbotts Law in the third house on the right. (The lane is just before a thatched cottage and almost opposite a trout farm.)

ABBOTTS LAW   **NEW**
Owners: Judith and David Pritchard
Abbotts Ann
Andover
Hampshire SPA 7DW
tel and fax: (01264) 710350
3 rooms with private bathrooms
From £21 per person
Open April to October
Children over 5

The Old Vicarage offers visitors an exceptionally delightful place to stay in this tranquil part of the country immortalized in Thomas Hardy's novels. Standing next to the old village church, surrounded by green lawns, neatly clipped hedges, and rose gardens, this fine Georgian house is owned by Anthea and Michael Hipwell who along with their black labrador Beeze offer a warm welcome to their gracious home. Breakfast is the only meal that Anthea prepares, but she has a long list of wonderful restaurants in the surrounding villages. Upstairs the bedrooms have pretty wallpapers and are furnished in tasteful English country style, in character with the decor throughout The Old Vicarage. There is a lot to see and do in the area: Cerne Abbas with its thatched cottage and giant carved into the hillside is the Casterbridge of Hardy's novels, and historic Dorchester, Salisbury, and Shaftesbury are nearby. The Dorset coast at Lulworth Cove, Durdle Door, and Ringstead Bay is a 20-minute drive. *Directions:* From Dorchester take the A35 northeast for 5 miles to Tolpuddle (this is the village where the six martyrs met to fight starvation farmworkers' wages) where you turn right for Affpuddle (1 mile).

THE OLD VICARAGE
Owners: Anthea and Michael Hipwell
Affpuddle
Dorchester
Dorset DT2 7HH
tel: (01305) 848315
3 rooms with private bathrooms
From £20 per person
Open all year
Children over 12

Tony and Sheila Sutton have converted this impressive house which was built as a vicarage in 1869, into a small hotel providing a centrally located, comfortable, hospitable base for exploring the Lake District. Bric-a-brac, capacious sofas, and an aspidistra in the window give a cluttered, Victorian air to the front lounge, though I would term the overall decor comfortably eclectic. Accommodation can be taken on a bed and breakfast basis, but guests usually opt for the dinner bed and breakfast rate because the Suttons make every effort to make dinner a special occasion. A typical menu might include warm smoked trout mousse with watercress and lemon, guinea fowl with walnuts and mushrooms, sticky toffee pudding, and cheese. Grey Friar is just a short distance from the bustling center of Ambleside. Whether you explore Lakeland by car or on foot you will find the scenery glorious: in spring the famous daffodils bloom, while in autumn the bracken and leaves turn a crisp, golden brown. At nearby Grasmere are Rydal Mount and Dove Cottage, poet William Wordsworth's homes. Hawkshead has a museum honoring Beatrix Potter and in Near Sawrey you can visit her home, Hill Top Farm, where she dreamed up such endearing characters as Mrs Tiggy Winkle and the Flopsy Bunnies. *Directions:* Grey Friar Lodge is 1.5 miles west of Ambleside on the A593, midway between Ambleside and Skelwith Bridge.

GREY FRIAR LODGE
Owners: Sheila and Tony Sutton
Clappersgate
Ambleside
Cumbria LA22 9NE
tel: (015394) 33158
8 rooms with private bathrooms
From £23.50 per person
Open March to October
Children over 12

Waterton Garden Cottage is part of a Victorian stable block that has been cleverly converted to two spacious homes. The house is set in a red-brick, walled garden of spacious lawns and flower beds with a heated swimming pool occupying a quiet corner beyond espaliered fruit trees. Ian, who has over 40 years experience in catering and hospitality and his wife, Mary, work as a team preparing dinner with Ian responsible for the main course and Mary concentrating on dessert. Guests are encouraged to bring their own wine to accompany the meal. What was once the tack-room is now a paneled dining room hung with framed photographs of tempting food dishes. A narrow, spiral staircase leads up to the guests' bedrooms (larger suitcases are not a problem as Ian transports them via the main staircase). Bedrooms are prettily decorated and each is accompanied by a modern, ensuite shower room. If you care for tea or coffee, just ask and it will be served to you in the drawing room. Waterton Garden Cottage is a quiet countryside spot where a short drive will bring you to the heart of Cirencester. Southern Cotswold villages such as Bibury with its beautiful old cottages are within easy reach. *Directions:* From Cirencester take the A417 (Lechlade road) for 2½ miles to Ampney Crucis. Turn right before the Crown of Crucis Hotel, signposted Driffield. Take the first farm track to the right and Waterton Garden Cottage is at the end (do not pull into the courtyard).

WATERTON GARDEN COTTAGE   **NEW**
Owners: Mary and Ian Cassidy
Ampney Crucis
Gloucestershire GL7 5RX
tel: (01285) 851303
3 rooms with private bathrooms
From £22.50 per person
Open all year
Children over 9
No Smoking house

Whenever Peter or Elizabeth Hartland see people peering curiously up their driveway they know they're Richmonds looking for their roots, for Cove House was the home of John Richmond who went with the men of Taunton to found Taunton, Massachusetts in 1640 and the Richmonds belong to the Richmond Society, a group who can trace their ancestors back to this wisteria-festooned manor house. Guests enjoy breakfast in the gracious dining room where lovely flower arrangements dress antique furniture. In the small adjacent study, an alcove lined with a detailed map of the area illustrates the many places of interest round and about: Avebury, Blenheim Palace, Oxford, Bath, and the Cotswold villages. The bedrooms are large and some can take an extra child's bed and cot. Nearby, flooded gravel pits which attract many species of waterfowl provide a birdwatcher's paradise. Peter, a retired schoolmaster, keeps informational brochures on hand for visitors' use and has also compiled a "good food guide" to local pubs and restaurants. Guests often walk the short distance into the village to eat at the White Hart or the Horse and Jockey. With advance notice Elizabeth is happy to prepare an evening meal for guests. *Directions:* The village of Ashton Keynes is 6 miles south of Cirencester. In the center of the village is the White Hart and 100 yards east a large wall bounds the driveway to Cove House. Drive through the inner gate.

COVE HOUSE
Owners: Major Peter and Elizabeth Hartland
2 Cove House
Ashton Keynes
Wiltshire SN6 6NS
tel: (01285) 861221
3 rooms with private bathrooms
From £24 per person
Closed Christmas and New Year
Children welcome
Wolsey Lodge

Austwick is a delightful village with a pub, post office-cum-general store, church, and a cluster of houses set against the background of the rolling limestone hills in the Three Peaks area of the Yorkshire Dales National Park. Just at the edge of the village green, Wood View, one of the village's larger houses, is home to Pam and Peter Taylor who used to run a nearby hotel before moving here. Their front door opens to a welcoming fire in the sitting room, just perfect for toasting your toes after a long day walking across the fells. Breakfast is the only meal served at the little tables in the low-beamed dining room and, while there's a pub just next door, guests often dine at the Cross Streets pub just a short drive away. The bedrooms are delightfully decorated in a very pleasing, unfussy way. I especially admired the two large front bedrooms and the attic bedroom with its massive support beam which tall folks have to duck under. The Settle to Carlisle railway is a great local attraction and Pam recommends that guests take the train as far as Appelby, where the gypsies hold their horse fair every June. Within an hour's leisurely drive you can be in the Lake District, the Trough of Bowland, Bronte Country, and the heart of the Yorkshire Dales. *Directions:* Driving from Skipton towards Kendal on the A65, turn right into Austwick village which is 4½ miles beyond Settle. Wood View is in the center of the village by the green.

WOOD VIEW   **NEW**
Owners: Pam and Peter Taylor
The Green
Austwick
Lancaster LA2 8BB
tel: (015242) 51268
5 rooms with private bathrooms
From £18 per person
Open Easter to October
Children over 5

The Barns is a comfortable spot to break a long journey between London and Edinburgh via the A1, or for a longer visit to explore Nottinghamshire. This county is famous not only for the exploits of Robin Hood, but also as the area where the Pilgrim Fathers formed their separatist church before setting sail for America and establishing a new colony. The Barns is the very tastefully converted hay and tractor barns of the next-door farm, and behind its redbrick facade all is spick and span. A sofa and chairs are drawn around a crackling log fire, and tables are topped with linen cloths neatly laid for breakfast. With advance notice Rosalie is happy to cook a traditional roast dinner. Upstairs the bedrooms are plainly decorated with cream walls highlighting dark beams and all have nice touches such as a fresh posy of flowers on a small antique dresser and elegant china tea cups. Room 1 is a particularly large family suite. A pleasant drive through Sherwood Forest brings visitors to the visitor center which has an exhibition on Robin Hood and his merry band and offers maps guiding you through ancient oaks trees to his former hideaways. Clumber Park near Sherwood Forest is noted for its main driveway planted with over 1,296 lime trees. *Directions:* From the south take the A1 north to the A57 (Worksop) roundabout, make a U turn and go south on the A1. Take the first left, on the B6420, towards Retford. The Barns is on the left.

THE BARNS
Owner: Rosalie Brammer
Morton Farm
Babworth, Retford
Nottinghamshire DN22 8HA
tel: (01777) 706336
6 rooms with private bathrooms
From £19 per person
Closed Christmas
Credit cards: EC, MC, VS
Children welcome

On a road of large, semi-detached Edwardian homes, Haydon House distinguishes itself as having the most colorful, pocket-sized garden. Magdalene has made the most of her home, decorating each of the rooms to perfection. Guests enjoy the sitting room with its plump sofas drawn cozily round the fire or the pocket-sized study with just enough room to spread your maps and books to plan the next day's adventures. The bedrooms are exceedingly pretty and named for the color of their decor: pink, green, blue, and peach. Request blue or peach if you want a more spacious room or room for a child's rollaway bed. With a choice of over 90 restaurants in the town, breakfast is the only meal served round the long, polished dining-room table and Magdalene offers a fresh fruit platter and several other alternatives to a traditional, cooked English breakfast. Bath with its graceful, honey-colored buildings, interesting museums, and superb shopping is best explored on foot over a period of several days. *Directions:* From Bath follow signs for and onto the A367 towards Exeter, pass an elongated roundabout by a railway viaduct, up a hill to a small shopping area, and onto a dual carriageway (The Bear pub is on your right). At the end of the shopping area fork right into Bloomfield Road and take the second right (by the telephone kiosk) into Bloomfield Park.

HAYDON HOUSE
Owners: Magdalene and Gordon Ashman
9 Bloomfield Park
Bath
Avon BA2 2BY
tel: (01225) 444919/427351
5 rooms with private bathrooms
From £27.50 per person
Open all year
Credit cards: all major
Children welcome
No Smoking house

Perched high above the city's rooftops, this large Victorian home offers every comfort for the visitor: luxurious bathrooms with heated towel rails and "perfect" showers, firm, American queen-sized beds, satellite television, in-house movies, picture-perfect decor, and the sincere attentions of Carrolle and George. Each of the bedrooms has its own flavor and, while I admired those in soft flowery pastels (the pink tower room with its lacy four-poster bed is very popular with honeymooners and there is a spacious ground-floor room for those who have difficulty with stairs), I particularly enjoyed the imaginative four-poster room where four turquoise obelisks are artfully draped in navy and white fabric to form the bedposts of this most interesting bed. Breakfast in the sunny green and yellow breakfast room offers lots of choices as well as the traditional English cooked breakfast. It's a 15-minute walk down into town. George has designed day-long driving tours that give detailed instructions for a full day's sightseeing so guests often venture as far afield as southern Wales. *Directions:* From Bath follows signs for and onto the A367 towards Exeter, pass an elongated roundabout by a railway viaduct, up a hill, and take the first turning to the right into Upper Oldfield Park. Holly Lodge is the first house on the right just past the bend.

HOLLY LODGE
Owners: Carrolle Sellick and George Hall
8 Upper Oldfield Park
Bath
Avon BA2 3JZ
tel: (01225) 424042/339187 fax: (01225) 481138
6 rooms with private bathrooms
From £37.50 per person
Open all year
Credit cards: all major
Children welcome
No Smoking house

Situated halfway up a steep hill, Somerset House is a classic Regency abode of warm, honey-colored stone, set in a spacious garden affording panoramic views of the city. The family pets (a parrot, dog and cat), along with family photos and books give a comfortable feeling to the Seymours' upscale guesthouse. Decorated in pastels, the bedrooms have matching drapes and bedspreads and whimsical rag dolls propped up on the pillows. Several rooms have an extra bed and a ground-floor room is ideal for those who have difficulty with stairs. Bedrooms are named after the sons and daughters of George III and in their note to guests Malcolm and Jean have included the child's historical particulars as well as the rules of the house. Jonathan and Jean specialize in delicious regional English cuisine. Saturday nights (not in the summer) are particularly special, for Jean plans a theme meal (on the night of our stay it was France), and gives a verbal rendition of the menu, explaining the origins of the dishes and their tempting contents. The basement dining room complements the food: light wood Windsor chairs, lace-topped tables, and a huge pine dresser set upon the checkerboard tile floor. A fifteen-minute walk brings you into the heart of Bath. *Directions:* Do not go into the city center, but follow signs for the University. Going up Bathwick Hill, Somerset House is on the left.

SOMERSET HOUSE
Owners: Jean, Malcolm, and Jonathan Seymour
35 Bathwick Hill
Bath
Avon BA2 6LD
tel: (01225) 466451/463471 fax: (01225) 317188
9 rooms with private bathrooms
From £31.00 per person
Open all year
Children over 10
No Smoking house

This listed Georgian country house is one of the many lovely homes in the conservation village of Bathford. The Orchard is set in its own walled grounds which feature sweeping lawns and a magnificent variety of old trees. It is difficult to believe that the bustling city of Bath is just fifteen minutes away from this tranquil spot. John and Olga London have a winning formula of a handsome house in beautiful surroundings, immaculately decorated and furnished with a tasteful mixture of fine antiques. Guests have full use of a very elegant yet very welcoming sitting room where a log fire blazes on chilly evenings and tall French doors and a large window open up to views of the perfectly groomed garden. Upstairs are three very generously proportioned, high-ceilinged bedrooms with large bay windows, discreetly placed televisions, and spacious bathrooms. The two front bedrooms have enviable views of an enormous copper beech tree, reputedly over 200 years old, and across the valley to green fields. The fourth bedroom, nicknamed The Folly, has a private garden entrance, lower ceilings, and small windows that overlook the garden. Guests who enjoy a country walk are directed across the orchard the nature reserve. Most guests stroll down the hill to dine at The Crown Inn. *Directions:* Leave the M4 at junction 18 and follow the A46 south to the A4 (towards Chippenham), turn right onto the A363 and left, at The Crown Inn, into Bathford. The Orchard is up the hill on the right, 200 yards beyond Bathford Post Office

THE ORCHARD
Owners: Olga and John London
Bathford
Bath
Avon BA1 7TG
tel: (01225) 858765
4 rooms with private bathrooms
From £27.50 per person
Open March to October
Children over 12

Frog Street Farm, a lovely gray, stone farmhouse dating back to 1436, is a real working farm where things are not fancy or cutesy pretty, but everything fits together perfectly with country freshness. From the moment you are met at the door by Veronica, with her true country-style warmth and jolly sense of humor, the mood is set. You are immediately made to feel part of the family and offered a cup of tea in front of the large inglenook fireplace before being shown to your room. The guestrooms are spotlessly clean and simply, but prettily, decorated with a color scheme of pinks and greens used throughout. Behind the house lies the farmyard while to the front is a colorful garden and a swimming pool shaded by a tall hedge. Veronica takes great pride in her cooking and, with advance notice, will prepare delicious meals from farm-fresh produce. For those who want to spend a few days in the country, away from city sophistication, Frog Street Farm is the epitome of what a farm vacation should be. In this pretty, rolling countryside are the charming little towns of Chard, Ilchester, Ilminster, and Crewkerne. To the north the limestone Mendip Hills are honeycombed with spectacular caves and gorges such as Wookey Hole and Cheddar Gorge. The magnificent cathedral city of Wells is within easy driving distance. *Directions:* From the M5 take exit 25 and continue 4½ miles southeast to Hatch Beauchamp. Take Station Road to Frog Street Farm.

FROG STREET FARM
Owner: Veronica Cole
Beercrocombe
Taunton
Somerset TA3 6AF
tel: (01823) 480430
3 rooms with private bathrooms
From £25 per person
Open March to October
Children over 12

I cannot guarantee that Drummond will take you for a ride on his miniature train but you might be lucky enough to take the quarter mile circuit of the 6-acre garden, past the front door, through a long tunnel and past the heated swimming pool. This makes Birchley seem like a theme park which it most certainly is not: it's a spectacular Tudor home whose former owners had visions of grandeur when they tacked on an enormous Edwardian addition which is now the house next door. There are three simply wonderful bedrooms, two with snug shower rooms and one with an enormous bath. Guests toast their toes in front of the log fire in the snug, oak-paneled sitting room and enjoy a hearty breakfast served on an ancient refectory table in the massive oak-beamed dining room with its glorious, carved oak inglenook. There are excellent pubs and restaurants within a few minutes' drive. This superb house merits a stay of several days—you can spend a week just touring gardens. Churchill's home, Chartwell, gives you a glimpse into the life of one of Britain's most famous politicians. Rye, Hastings, Dover, and Canterbury are popular destinations. *Directions:* Leave the M20 at junction 8 following signs for Leeds Castle. In 4 miles turn left at the Plough Inn in the direction of Tenterden. After 6 miles, turn right at the green in Biddenden (Tunbridge Wells), and after 1 mile turn left (opposite the garden center) and Birchley is on your left.

BIRCHLEY
Owners: Jennifer and Drummond Randall
Fosten Green Lane
Biddenden
Ashford
Kent TH27 8DZ
tel: (01580) 291413   fax: (01580) 291413
3 rooms with private bathrooms
From £30 per person
Closed Christmas and New Year
Children over 10

Appletree Holme Farm sits in a fold of the hills surrounded by tumbling moorlands. It's an isolated spot yet just a few miles from the busy heart of the Lake District. After running a large hotel, Roy and Shirley came here several years ago to create a small establishment that they could operate themselves. Roy does the cooking, offering a set four-course dinner that may include Lakeland lamb roasted with rosemary as a main course. After dinner guests peruse the extensive breakfast menu, and make their selections from fruit salad, traditional grills, smoked fish, egg dishes, and porridge so that Roy can have breakfast hot and ready for the time of their choosing. The living rooms are snug and cozy, with open fires and lots of books. Upstairs Shirley decided to give guests something they would not have at home, consequently The Blue Room boasts a huge bathroom with a large circular bubble tub sitting center stage beneath an ornate chandelier and The Orchard Room has a large free-standing circular shower in the bedroom. The adjacent Down House, which I was unable to see because it was occupied, has its own entrance and private garden. Within a few miles are some of the Lake District's best-known villages, Coniston, Hawkshead, Sawrey, and Ambleside. *Directions:* Blawith is halfway between Coniston and Ulverston on the A5084. Take the lane opposite the village church, after ½ mile turn right, and in another ½ mile turn left.

APPLETREE HOLME FARM
Owners: Shirley and Roy Carlsen
Blawith
Ulverston
Cumbria LA12 8EL
tel: (01229) 885618
4 rooms with private bathrooms
From £60 per person dinner, B and B
Open all year
Credit cards: all major
Children by arrangement

This well-proportioned Victorian rectory is set in secluded grounds overlooking glorious vistas of the Derbyshire countryside. Geraldine and Stuart Worthington's solicitous welcome includes an invitation to the evening dinner party. Guests are introduced to each other over cocktails in the drawing room before sitting down to the large dining-room table, beautifully laid with silver and crystal. Geraldine and Stuart dine with their guests; Geraldine serving unobtrusively with Stuart pouring the wine. After dinner, guests, host, and hostess return to the drawing room for port and coffee around the cheery log fire. The front bedroom has a large double bed framed by blue and white flowered draperies hung from a coronet, matching bedspread and bed ruffle, and an ensuite bathroom. The large twin room has thick bathrobes so guests can pop across the hall to their bathroom. The third twin room tucked under the eaves of the roof has a steeply sloping ceiling and adjacent luxurious shower room. The dramatic and rugged Derbyshire scenery is a strong attraction for walkers. Many visitors also tour Chatsworth House, Haddon Hall, and the open-air Monday market in Bakewell. *Directions:* Leave Ashbourne on the A523 towards Leek. After 2 miles turn right towards Ilam. Drive through Okeover Park and turn left as you go through the gates. After 2 miles, at Blore crossroads, turn left and The Old Rectory is on your right beyond the church.

THE OLD RECTORY
Owners: Geraldine and Stuart Worthington
Blore, Ashbourne
Derbyshire DE CBS
tel and fax: (01335) 350287
3 rooms with private bathrooms
From £36 per person
Credit cards: EC, MC, VS
Closed Christmas
Children not accepted
Wolsey Lodge

With its back nestled against woodland, Boldre Hill faces out across rolling countryside to the distant coast and the Isle of Wight. Spacious, high-ceilinged rooms and broad hallways characterize this large home where Anna Morris, in the Wolsey Lodge tradition, welcomes guests as friends. On chilly days the fire in the drawing room provides a cheery warmth. In summer, guests often relax under the wisteria on the terrace. Guests dine together round a lovely old table that fits snugly at one end of the dining room, leaving plenty of room for sofas and a television at the other. The principal bedroom enjoys a large bathroom and a huge bay window that frames the countryside view. Two very attractive, twin-bedded rooms face the woodlands at the rear of the house. Just up the lane there's walking, riding, and pony-watching in the New Forest. The sea is close by with lovely walks along the beaches. A ferry sails from nearby Lymington to the Isle of Wight. If you are interested in cars, be sure to visit the world-famous motor museum at Beaulieu. *Directions:* From Bockenhurst railway crossing, on the A337, continue for 2½ miles towards Lymington, turn left at the signpost for Boldre and Pilley (not the turning to Boldre church) and Boldre Hill is on your right, opposite the entrance to Hill House School.

BOLDRE HILL   **NEW**
Owner: Anna Morris
Rope Hill
Boldre
Lymington
Hampshire SO41 8ND
tel: (01590) 672614
3 rooms with private bathrooms
From £29 per person
Closed Christmas
Children welcome
Wolsey Lodge

9-6-96

Kath and Tony Peacock enjoy nothing more than singing with their church choir which is so noted for its musical prowess that it travels to Europe and America to give concerts. How appropriate with their ecclesiastical connection that they live in what was Boltongate's large, rambling, Victorian rectory. Tony loves to cook and stays busy in the kitchen while Kath has pre-dinner drinks with guests in the colorfully decorated drawing room. In contrast to the tall-ceilinged, large-windowed rooms of the rectory, the dining room dates back to the 16th century and has a low-beamed ceiling and a large inglenook fireplace with a wood-burning stove. Here guests dine together by lamplight, feasting on Anthony's specialties. Bedrooms are large and comfortable, decorated with pretty wallpapers and matching drapes. Two have ensuite bathrooms while the largest has its bathroom (robes provided) down the hall. Boltongate is on the quiet, northernmost fringes of the Lake District, a perfect spot to break a journey to or from Scotland. Pretty towns and villages abound such as Caldbeck, Borrowdale, Ullswater, and Buttermere. William Wordsworth's birthplace is nearby in Cockermouth. *Directions:* Leave the M6 at exit 40, bypass Keswick and take the A591 for 7 miles. At the Castle Inn turn right at the sign for Ireby. The Old Rectory is the first house in the village on your right.

THE OLD RECTORY
Owners: Kathleen and Anthony Peacock
Boltongate
Cumbria CA5 1DA
tel: (016973) 71647 fax: (016973) 71798
3 rooms with private bathrooms
From £33.50 per person
Closed December to March
Credit cards: EC, MC, VS
Children over 14
No Smoking house
Wolsey Lodge

Great food!
Delightful hosts —

When the tide is out you can drive around Bosham harbor, but heed the flooding signs well for, as the photographs in the Blue Anchor pub attest, cars that are left parked are submerged to their rooftops by the incoming tide which leaves them gaily draped in seaweed as it ebbs. From the outside, Hatpins looks like a well-kept suburban home, attractive but not especially different from other residences on the street. However, once inside, you will find this is a very smart place because the owner, Mary Waller, has combined her talent as a seamstress with a natural flair for decorating to transform her home into a delightfully inviting bed and breakfast. Her talents are displayed in every room of the house in the drapes, pillows, and bed coverings which she has skillfully sewn from lovely fabrics. Two bedrooms are behind the house and enjoy a private entrance and sunny patio. Bosham brims with charm: it is great fun to wander down to the waterfront and explore the tiny lanes. Be sure not to miss the old church (depicted in the Bayeux Tapestry) where King Canute's daughter is buried. The nearby Roman palace at Fishbourne is a great attraction as are the ships *HMS Victory, Mary Rose*, and *HMS Warrior* in nearby Portsmouth. *Directions:* From Chichester take the A259 west for 3 miles to Bosham. Hatpins is on the main road into town.

HATPINS
Owner: Mary Waller
Bosham Lane
Bosham
Chichester
Sussex PO18 8HG
tel: (01243) 572644
4 rooms with private bathrooms
From £25 per person
Open all year
Children welcome
No Smoking house

Visitors come to Pethills Bank Cottage to visit the sights in the region, then return because this bed and breakfast is the most delightful place to stay. Set high on a hill surrounded by fields, the cottage sits snug in an acre of rolling gardens overlooking the countryside. The cozy living room has thick, golden stone walls and a large picture window framing the rolling lawn and rockery garden. The bedrooms are unexpectedly large, decorated in an unobtrusive, modern style which gives them a light, airy, and uncluttered feel. Each has an ensuite bathroom and a host of extras: biscuit jar brimming with tempting goodies, fruit bowl, mineral water, iron, hairdryer, remote control television, shampoo, and bath oil. The Garden Room, decorated in pretty greens and creams, opens up to a verandah which overlooks the fields, The Dales Room also has magnificent countryside views and the largest bathroom. The Cottage Room has old-world charm with a beamed ceiling and low windows. Breakfast fortifies you for the entire day as it includes an array of fruits, crisp bacon, sausage, eggs, tomatoes, and mushrooms, and toast with homemade jam and marmalade. Yvonne helps guests plan visits to the Potteries factories and seconds shops (for example, Coalport, Royal Doulton, Minton, Spode, and Wedgwood). Derbyshire's dales and historic houses are close at hand. *Directions:* Bottomhouse is on the A523 between Leek and Ashbourne. Turn into the lane opposite the Little Chef restaurant and follow the signs up the hill for about a mile.

PETHILLS BANK COTTAGE
Owners: Yvonne and Richard Martin
Bottomhouse, Leek
Staffordshire ST13 7PF
tel: (01538) 304277/304555 fax: (01538) 304575
3 rooms with private bathrooms
From £19 per person
Closed Christmas
Children welcome

This exquisite home takes its name from the Bourne Eau stream that runs alongside its grounds, separating it from an ancient abbey and a park. This house has evolved over the years and Dawn and George Bishop have decorated each room according to its historical period. The Elizabethan dining room has a flagstone floor topped with an Oriental carpet and a trestle table set before a huge inglenook fireplace beneath a low-beamed ceiling. The high-ceilinged, formal Georgian drawing room has enviable antiques and the snug Jacobean music room has a concert piano and a cheery log fire blazing in the ornately carved fireplace. Guests enjoy a scrumptious cooked breakfast in the low-ceilinged breakfast room furnished in mellow country pine. Bedrooms are equally lovely: the enormous Master Suite has a large sitting area around a fireplace whose mantle was once part of the abbey's altar and an adjacent dressing room with a single bed; the smaller Jacobean Room with its period bed has a glorious modern bathroom; and the large twin-bedded Georgian Room has a private staircase and views across the vast lawns. Many guests visit Burghley House, Belton House, Belvoir Castle, and Stamford where the film *Middlemarch* was filmed. Gently rolling wolds lead north to Lincoln with its cobbled streets, majestic hilltop cathedral, and castle. *Directions:* Bourne is on the A15 between Peterborough and Sleaford. The concealed entrance is on the A15, 200 yards south of the main traffic lights in the middle of town, opposite the park.

BOURNE EAU HOUSE
Owners: Dawn and George Bishop
Bourne
Lincolnshire PE10 9LY
tel: (01778) 423621
3 rooms with private bathrooms
From £30 per person
Closed Christmas
Children welcome
Wolsey Lodge

Willmead Farm is a wonderfully endearing thatched cottage nestled in a sheltered glen: a perfectly idyllic setting. Willmead has three simply decorated bedrooms grouped around a minstrels' gallery that overlooks the entrance hall. The twin-bedded room has an ensuite bathroom while the two doubles share the facilities of two bathrooms. Low-beamed ceilings and old-fashioned board doors with metal latches add to the appeal of this storybook house. Comfortable sofas and chairs are grouped around the fireplace in the sitting room and beyond is the dining room where guests gather in the morning around the large table. A scrumptious farmhouse breakfast that includes homemade jams is the only meal that Hilary serves. However, Hilary has compiled a book of local restaurants' menus so guests can choose where to dine. For a sinfully rich Devon cream tea, detour round the duck pond and follow the path that leads past the barn to the thatched hamlet of Lustleigh. The wild beauty of Dartmoor with its sheltered villages and market towns, wild ponies, and spectacular scenery is a magnet for walkers and those touring by car. *Directions:* From Exeter take the A38 towards Plymouth and exit at the A382 but do not go into Bovey Tracey: stay on the A382 Lustleigh road. After 2 miles you pass a phone box on your right and take the first narrow lane on the left for half a mile to Willmead.

WILLMEAD FARM
Owner: Hilary Roberts
Bovey Tracey
Newton Abbot
Devon TQ13 9NP
tel: (016477) 214
3 rooms, 1 with private bathroom
From £22 per person
Closed Christmas
Children over 10
No Smoking house

Pickett Howe is a picture-perfect, whitewashed farmhouse nestled amongst green fields beneath rugged Lakeland peaks. As you drive into the farmyard, Rowan, a golden retriever, bounds over to greet you with enthusiastic tail-wagging and smiles. And, best of all, the interior lives up to all the promise of the exterior: there are polished slate floors topped with Oriental rugs, heavy oak beams, and small stone-mullioned windows set deep in thick stone walls. Settled down on the sofa chatting with David and Dani over tea and homemade cakes, you soon feel thoroughly at home. Upstairs the four little bedrooms are tucked neatly under the eaves. All have Victorian brass and wrought-iron beds, three have Jacuzzi bathtubs (and showers), while the fourth has a shower. Dani loves to cook and produces sumptuous dinners where there is always a choice of meat, fish or vegetarian for the main course: small wonder that rigorous walking is often the order of the day (the upstairs parlor is well stocked with information from Wainwright's guides to Ordinance Survey maps). Meander across Brackenthwaite Howe to sit quietly by Crummock Water (the Edwards have the National Trust boathouse key) or stride up Grasmoor. *Directions:* From exit 40 on the M6 take the A66 past Keswick, and turn left onto the B5292 to Lorton. Then follow signs for Buttermere. After 2 miles take the left fork (B5289) for Buttermere and the entrance to Pickett Howe is on your right after 1/3 mile.

PICKETT HOWE
Owners: Dani and David Edwards
Brackenthwaite, Buttermere Valley
Cumbria CA13 9UY
tel: (01900) 85444
4 bedrooms with private bathrooms
From £35 per person
Credit cards EC, MC, VS
Open April to mid-November
Children over 10
No Smoking house

Priory Steps, a row of 17th-century weavers' cottages high above the town of Bradford on Avon, is a glorious place to stay. The village tumbles down the hill to the banks of the River Avon, its narrow streets full of interesting shops and antique dealers. A few miles distant, the glories of Bath await exploration and are easily accessible by car or the local train service. Hostess Diana is a gourmet cook and guests dine en famille in the traditionally furnished dining room. While Diana's cooking is reason enough to spend several days here, the adjacent library with its books and pamphlets highlighting the many places to visit in the area provides additional justification. The bedrooms are all very different, each accented with antique furniture, and each has a smart modern bathroom, television, and tea and coffee tray. The Blue Room has large shuttered and curtained windows and a pleasing decor in shades of blue, while the large English Room has striped paper in muted tones of green coordinating with flowered curtains. There is a touch of whimsy in the bathroom of the dark-beamed Frog Room where the odd frog or two has inspired former guests to send their own contributions to an ever-growing collection of the creatures. The frogless bedroom itself is very pretty. *Directions:* Take the A363 from Bath to Bradford on Avon. As the road drops steeply into the town, Newtown is the first road to the right. Priory Steps is 150 yards on the left.

PRIORY STEPS
Owners: Diana and Carey Chapman
Newtown
Bradford on Avon
Wiltshire BA15 1NQ
tel: (01225) 862230   fax: (01225) 866248
5 rooms with private bathrooms
From £28 per person
Open all year
Children over 12
Wolsey Lodge

The heart of the Lake District is often bustling with visitors so you may prefer to stay with Enid and Hugh Davies in a less commercialized area, make driving forays to the famous beauty spots, and return in the evening to the peace and quiet of Low Hall. Hugh is an anesthetist and Enid was a teacher until she saw Low Hall while house-hunting and decided to put her entertaining skills to work running a guesthouse. Enid says it is like having a house party every night. Guests dine by candlelight in the quaint, beamed dining room (the five-course dinner offers a choice of meat, fish, or vegetarian for the main course) and retire to the comfortable sitting room for coffee, fudge, and a chat. There is plenty of room for the large brass bed in the flowery Victorian Bedroom. The other four flowery guestrooms are smaller, with snug shower rooms tucked into a corner. A 3-mile walk along the riverbank brings you to Cockermouth, William Wordsworth's birthplace. Over Whinlatter Pass lies Keswick, a bustling little town at the heart of the Lake District. An hour's drive enables you to visit the forts along Hadrian's Wall. *Directions:* From exit 40 on the M6 take the A66 to Cockermouth and turn left onto the A5086 for 1 mile to the school where you turn left towards Lorton. Low Hall is on your right after 1 mile.

LOW HALL
Owners: Enid and Hugh Davies
Brandlingill
Cockermouth
Cumbria CA13 0RE
tel: (01900) 826654
5 rooms with private bathrooms
From £20 per person
Open March to November
Children over 10
No Smoking house

Deep in the Devon countryside, in a 16th-century stone and cob farmhouse called Lower Beers, Anne Nicholls has realized her dream and founded Bonne Bouche, a residential cooking school. Here she and her husband Gerald provide guests an idyllic spot to perfect their culinary skills. Course offerings range from weekends designed to remove the angst from entertaining to an in-depth four-week course. Her approach is both creative and practical, a handy combination. The Nicholls also welcome guests who are simply on holiday, spending their days exploring the lush Devon countryside and enjoying delicious candlelit dinners in the evenings. The comfortable sitting room offers guests an inviting sofa and chairs in front of the enormous fireplace as well as an assortment of books and magazines. Bedrooms are named after herbs and are fresh and clean, with flower-sprigged bedcovers and matching draperies or wallpapers. Some sightseeing options are to explore Dartmoor and Exmoor and to visit the National Trust properties of Knightshayes and Killerton. *Directions:* Lower Beers is only five minutes from the motorway. Leave the M5 at exit 28 and turn into Cullompton. At the first T junction turn right towards Willand on the B3181. In 1 mile, just before the pylons, turn left to Brithem Bottom. Lower Beers is the second house on the left after 1 mile.

LOWER BEERS
Owners: Anne and Gerald Nicholls
Brithem Bottom
Cullompton
Devon EX15 1NB
tel: (01884) 32257 fax: (01884) 32257
4 rooms with private bathrooms
From £30 per person
Closed Christmas
Children over 14
No Smoking house
Wolsey Lodge

Gently rolling hills where sheep graze peacefully and shaded valleys with meandering streams surround the picturesque village of Broad Campden where The Malt House hugs the quiet main street. Years ago barley was made into malt here for brewing beer. Now it is a picturesque, very up-market bed and breakfast that provides a perfect central location for exploring other Cotswold villages. A quiet sitting room invites browsing through books and magazines. If requested in advance, dinner or lunch are served on a long table before a massive inglenook fireplace and mullioned windows which offer glimpses of the orchard beyond the garden. All the bedrooms except a small single room face the garden, so guests are ensured a quiet night's repose. The rooms all have plenty of country-cottage charm and several have delightful bathrooms with old-fashioned Victorian tubs. One has a lovely four poster bed while another is a delightful suite with a sitting room and bedrooms set beneath the eaves up a narrow staircase. Lovely Cotswold villages to explore include Chipping Campden, Bourton-on-the-Water, Upper and Lower Slaughter, Stow-on-the-Wold, Bibury, and Broadway. Garden lovers will enjoy Kiftsgate, Hidcote Manor, and Batsford. *Directions:* On entering Chipping Campden take the first right: you know you are in Broad Campden when you see The Bakers Arms. The Malt House is opposite the wall topped by a tall topiary hedge.

THE MALT HOUSE
Owners: Jean and Nick Brown
Broad Campden
Chipping Campden
Gloucestershire GL55 6UU
tel: (01386) 840295 fax: (01386) 841334
5 rooms with private bathrooms
From £39.50 per person
Closed Christmas
Children welcome

Just up the lane from the Malt House (our other Broad Campden listing) sits Orchard Hill House, the lovely, mellow-stone, farmhouse home of Caroline and David Ashmore and their two young children. Their low-beamed dining room sits at the center of the house and it is here that guests gather in the morning to enjoy breakfast round the long trestle table before the large inglenook fireplace. Upstairs are two delightfully decorated bedrooms, one with a snug ensuite shower room and the other with its private Victorian-style bathroom across the hall. While the rooms in the main farmhouse are very nice I really enjoyed the privacy of going up the barn's stone staircase to the lofty, beamed Hayloft. Here you have a spacious room with a sitting area and twin and double beds. An adjacent twin-bedded room is set snugly beneath the barn's low beams. For dinner Caroline directs guests to the Bakers Arms in the village or makes suggestions from amongst the many excellent pubs, restaurants and bistros in nearby Chipping Campden. Neighboring Snowshill is famous for its toy collection. The beautiful gardens of Kiftsgate and Hidcote are on the way to Stratford-upon-Avon which is just 10 miles away. *Directions:* On entering Chipping Campden take the first right. Pass the Bakers Arms pub and the Malt House, and Orchard Hill House is the next house on your left.

ORCHARD HILL HOUSE   **NEW**
Owners: Caroline and David Ashmore
Broad Campden
Chipping Campden
Gloucestershire GL55 6UU
tel: (01386) 841473
4 rooms with private bathrooms
From £21 per person
Closed Christmas
Children over 2
No Smoking house

Luigi Bellorini came to England many years ago to learn the language. It took him longer than he thought and, while struggling to conjugate his verbs, he fell in love with an English girl, married, and made Britain his home. The desire to cook his national food in his own restaurant lingered and after his children were grown, Luigi and his wife Pauline took the plunge, moved to Broadway, and added an airy conservatory restaurant to this characterful 400-year-old house. Now every evening Luigi can be found in his kitchen creating his culinary magic, while still finding time to visit tables and have a special little chat with each of his patrons. Italian food lovers will be delighted by both the set and a-la-carte menus, though it must be emphasized that the menu is not limited to Italian food nor the wine list to Italian wines. After a delightful dinner and a nightcap in the residents' bar, guests stroll the quiet streets of Broadway before retiring to their rooms up the narrow staircase or across the courtyard. Bedrooms are not fancy but they are prettily decorated and each has its own tiny ensuite shower or bathroom. Guests who are staying longer than a couple of nights particularly enjoy the courtyard room for they can come and go as they have their own private entrance. A stay at Milestone House allows you to enjoy picturesque Broadway in the less crowded hours of early morning and evening. *Directions:* Broadway is on the A44 between Evesham and Stow-on-the-Wold.

MILESTONE HOUSE
Owners: Pauline and Luigi Bellorini
122 High Street
Broadway
Worcestershire WR12 7AJ
tel: (01386) 853432
4 rooms with private bathrooms
From £28.50 per person (no singles)
Closed Christmas
Credit cards: EC, MC, VS
Children welcome

In summer blowzy hollyhocks frame the door of College House, a substantial, 17th-century home fronting a quiet street just off the village green of this quiet Cotswold village. Old flagstones cover the floors, the walls are a soft pastel colorwash, and whimsical stenciling adds decorative interest to the shutters and the old fireplace which displays Sybil's collection of antique bottles. Nothing is cluttered or over-decorated. Sybil used to own a restaurant and is happy with advanced notice to provide a three-course dinner. The main bedroom has a huge, luxurious bathroom decked out in blue and white; the bedroom is equally large, with a sleigh bed sitting center stage and an interesting priest hole with a small circular window and stencils of dwarf orange trees in tubs on the walls. Pale lemon bows decorate the draperies and bed linen of The Yellow Room, blending beautifully with the soft lemon-colored walls. The slipper tub in the bathroom is perfect for those who enjoy a deep soak and a read. The third bedroom is less expensive because its bathroom is up a spiraling wooden staircase in the attic. While guests visit Bath, Oxford, and Stratford-upon-Avon, Sybil finds what they enjoy most is following her tape that tours them through lesser-known Cotswold villages. *Directions:* From Stow-on-the-Wold take the A429 towards Moreton in Marsh. Turn right signposted Broadwell and Evenlode. College House is on your left on the Evenlode side of the village.

COLLEGE HOUSE
Owner: Sybil Gisby
Chapel Street
Broadwell, Moreton in Marsh
Gloucestershire GL56 0TW
tel: (01451) 832351
3 rooms with private bathrooms
From £19.50 per person
Open all year
Children over 16

The Buck Inn is a traditional Georgian coaching inn. It stands beneath the towering craggy heights of Buckden Pike which rises steeply behind the inn. Conviviality and good cheer are the order of the day in the bar where real ale is hand-pulled from the cool stone cellars. In summer there is always a crowd and overnight guests may prefer the quieter restaurant in a bright, enclosed courtyard where in days of old sheep auctions were held. You can enjoy a set, four-course dinner with lots of choices for each course or order from the extensive bar menu offering salads, sandwiches, grills, fish, homemade pies, and traditional English fare. Upstairs bedrooms are far more attractive than the mediocre ones on the ground floor. Bedrooms are country-style in their decor, the largest being a four-poster room with a high, raftered ceiling. The surrounding rugged countryside offers many paths for walkers whether they prefer long day hikes or shorter strolls. Wharfedale has several lovely, mellow, stone villages such as Grassington, Appletreewick, and Kettlewell. It is a spectacular drive from here through Coverdale to Middleham with its ruined castle and on to Jervaulx with its romantic ruined abbey. To the west, moorland roads lead to Arncliffe and Littondale and on to Malham (in Airedale), famous for its massive crags, tarn, and cove. *Directions:* Buckden is 18 miles north of Skipton on the B6160.

THE BUCK INN
Owners: Marjorie and Roy Hayton
Buckden
Skipton
Yorkshire, BD23 5JA
tel: (01756) 760228 fax: (01756) 760227
14 rooms with private bathrooms
From £35 per person
Open all year
Credit cards: EC, MC, VS
Children welcome

Butlers is a 17th-century farmhouse sitting in secluded countryside, ideally located for touring the pretty villages and churches of Suffolk and Essex. Butlers' exterior is covered with traditional pargettry (ornamental plasterwork) while the inside is all beams and cottagey rooms. Guests enjoy a comfortable sitting room with a piano and a small television. Sylvia is happy to provide a dinner that can range from a simple supper to a more elaborate, three-course meal or she helps guests choose from several restaurants and pubs within a 10-mile radius. Upstairs, the bedrooms come in three sizes. A snug double and twin-bedded room share a bathroom. A larger beamed room has an ensuite bathroom. The biggest, an L-shaped double room enjoys a large bed and an ensuite bathroom with the bathtub, loo, and washbasin tucked into an alcove beside the bed. Colchester, the oldest recorded town in England (with its museum, libraries, and art galleries) is 9 miles away. Sudbury (6 miles) offers Gainsborough's birthplace and museum, while Constable's Flatford Mill lies across the valley. Antique shops abound in Long Melford, Clare, and Lavenham. *Directions:* Bures is on the B1508 between Colchester and Sudbury. From Sudbury cross the river into Bures Hamlet. Bear right on the left hand bend, under the railway bridge, and turn immediately left into Colne Road. Butlers is on your left after 1 mile.

BUTLERS   **NEW**
Owners: Sylvia and Paul Roberts
Colne Road
Bures Hamlet
Bures
Suffolk CO8 5DN
tel: (01787) 227243
3 rooms with private bathrooms
From £19 per person
Closed Christmas
Children over 5

The clomp of hooves as horses pulled carriages down the main street of Burford has long disappeared, but the inns that provided lodging and food to weary travelers remain and if you are in search of a simple, quaint hostelry, you can do no better than to base yourself at The Lamb for the duration of your Cotswold stay. A tall, upholstered settle sits before the fireplace on the flagstone floor of the main room, the hall table displays gleaming brass jelly molds, and an air of times long past pervades the place, particularly in winter when the air is heavy with the scent of woodsmoke and a flickering fire burns in the grate. Narrow staircases and corridors zigzag up and down to the little bedrooms, all simply decorated in a charming cottagey style. In the dining room the four-course dinner menu, with lots of choices for each course, is priced according to what is selected for the main course. The homely little bar with its stone-flagged floor and wooden settles has an indefinable mixture of character and atmosphere. Burford's main street is bordered by numerous antique, gift, and tea shops. There are mellow stone Cotswold villages to explore and Blenheim Palace and Oxford are less than an hour's drive away. *Directions:* Burford is midway between Oxford and Cheltenham (A40). The Lamb Inn is on Sheep Street, just off the village center.

THE LAMB INN
Owners: Caroline and Richard De Wolf
Sheep Street
Burford
Oxfordshire OX18 4LR
tel: (01993) 823155
15 rooms
From £40 per person
Open all year
Credit cards: EC, MC, VS
Children welcome

Built over a century ago, Chilvester Hill House is a solidly constructed Victorian home isolated from the busy A4 by a large garden. John and Gill Dilley retired here and subsequently unretired themselves: John, a physician, now works as an occupational health consultant and Gill entertains guests and breeds beef cattle. Gill enjoys cooking and a typical (optional) dinner might consist of smoked trout, lamb noisettes with vegetables from the garden, fruit fool, and cheese and biscuits. They have a short wine list with over twenty French and German wines. A soft pastel decor, treasured antiques, and a cleverly displayed collection of commemorative plates make the large, high-ceilinged drawing room the most elegant room in the house. The bedrooms are spacious, high-ceilinged rooms, each individually decorated with flowery Sanderson wallpaper. All have mineral water, tea and coffee tray, television, tourist information, and private bathroom. Visitors can enjoy the heated swimming pool during the summer months or take advantage of John and Gill's mimeographed maps marked with scenic routes to nearby Castle Combe, Lacock, and the Avebury Neolithic Circle. Bath, Oxford, and Salisbury are an easy drive away. *Directions:* From London leave the M4 at junction 14 and follow signs for Hungerford. Turn right on the A4 through Marlborough to Calne. Follow Chippenham signs for ½ mile, turn right (Bremhill) and immediately right into the drive.

CHILVESTER HILL HOUSE
Owners: Gill and John Dilley
Calne
Wiltshire SN11 0LP
tel: (01249) 813981   fax: (01249) 814217
3 rooms with private bathrooms
From £30 per person
Open all year
Credit cards: all major
Children over 12
Wolsey Lodge

Because of its quiet country location just 3 miles off the motorway, almost equidistant between Edinburgh and London, New Capernwray Farm is an ideal place to break a long, tiring journey. However, many weary travelers return for a proper country getaway to explore this unspoiled area. There really is nothing "new" about this solid, whitewashed stone farmhouse, for despite its name, it is approaching its 300th birthday. It was bought in 1974 by Sally and Peter Townend, who supervised its complete refurbishment while preserving its lovely old features, and now offer a very warm welcome to their guests. Before dinner you enjoy sherry in the cozy sitting room in front of a cheerful fire and then proceed to the dining room for a candlelit dinner. Bedrooms are particularly light, bright, and cheerful in their decor. The largest bedroom spans the breadth of the house, has a bathroom tucked neatly under the eaves and, as in all the rooms, is well equipped with tea, coffee, biscuits, television, hairdryer, mints, and a substantial sewing kit. A twin-bedded room has an ensuite shower room and the double bedded room has its shower room down the hall. Peter and Sally offer guided tours and have a wealth of books and maps on the Lake District, and the Yorkshire Dales. *Directions:* Leave the M6 at junction 35 and from the roundabout follow signs for Over Kellet. Turn left at the T junction into Over Kellet. Turn left at the village green: after 2 miles the farm is on the left.

NEW CAPERNWRAY FARM
Owners: Sally and Peter Townend
Capernwray
Carnforth
Lancashire LA6 1AD
tel and fax: (01524) 734284
3 rooms with private bathrooms
From £27.50 per person
Closed Christmas
Children over 10
Wolsey Lodge

Thruxted Oast, conveniently located about a 10-minute drive south of Canterbury, like so many fine old buildings, was in a most dilapidated condition before being rescued by Hilary and Tim Derouet and transformed into a lovely home. The ground floor has a dining room and a parlor, but the heart of the house is the family-style kitchen where guests gather each morning at a large antique farmhouse table for a delicious breakfast. Upstairs the three guest bedrooms are cleverly converted from the three original drying stalls with their high-peaked wooden ceilings and massive rafters. These spacious, twin-bedded rooms are attractively papered with a tiny print design which is complemented by pretty, short drapes at the windows. The same pattern is repeated in the handmade patchwork quilts, throw pillows, and dressing table skirts: my favorite room, Chaucer, features soft pink and green tones. Tim used to be a farmer and evidence of his green thumb can be seen in the lovely garden stretching behind the oast where abundant flowers border a verdant, green lawn. Canterbury is 4 miles away. *Directions:* From Canterbury take the A28 towards Ashford. On the city outskirts cross the A2 and after 200 yards turn left on St Nicholas Road. At the end T junction, turn right. Continue 2 miles, past St Augustine Hospital. Continue straight over the cross road and down the hill to Thruxted Oast on the right.

THRUXTED OAST
Owners: Hilary and Tim Derouet
Chartham
Canterbury
Kent CT4 7BX
tel: (01227) 730080
3 rooms with private bathrooms
From £37.50 per person
Closed Christmas
Credit cards: all major
Children over 12

9-2-96

Theresa White, who hails from Edinburgh, prides herself on offering a warm Scottish welcome to her up-market bed-and-breakfast hotel located a brisk 20-minute walk from the heart of medieval Chester. When she bought Redlands in the 1980s it was very different from the flower-decked, frothily Victorian establishment that you find today. Theresa has kept all the lovely woodwork and ornate plasterwork, adding modern bathrooms, central heating, vast quantities of sturdy Victorian furniture, four suits of armor, and masses of Victorian bric-a-brac. Guests help themselves to drinks at the honesty bar and relax in the sumptuous drawing room which includes among its array of furniture high-backed armchairs which almost surround you. Traditional Scottish porridge is a must when you order breakfast in the dining room where little tables are covered with starched Victorian tablecloths. For dinner Theresa is happy to advise on where to eat in town. Pay the few extra pounds and request one of the "best" rooms, for not only are they more spacious, but you will be treated to a lovely old bed (with modern mattress, of course) and decor where everything from the draperies to the china is color-coordinated. Walking round Chester's Roman walls is a good way to orient yourself to the city. It is fun to browse in The Rows, double-decker layers of shops. *Directions:* Redlands Hotel is located on the A5104 1 mile from the city center.

REDLANDS HOTEL   **NEW**
Owner: Theresa White
64 Hough Green
Chester CH4 8JY
tel: (01244) 671024 fax: (01244) 681309
12 rooms with private bathrooms
From £25 per person
Open all year
Credit cards: AX
Children over 2

nice washing faculties — A BIT NOISY

Chiddingfold, with its attractive homes set round the village green, is one of the most picturesque villages on the wooded Surrey Downs. A dovecote fronts the country lane just off the village green and a path leads beside it through a picture-book English cottage garden to Greenaway, the charming home of Sheila and John Marsh. The interior is just as delightful as the exterior, with low-ceilinged, beamed rooms, each decorated to perfection without making them stiffly formal or contrived. Guests enjoy the lovely living room with its views of the garden and part of Sheila and John's collection of colorful Staffordshire pottery displayed on the mantleshelf above the massive fireplace. Breakfast is served in the cozy dining room or, if guests prefer to sit and chat, they can eat their breakfast at the trestle table in the kitchen. For dinner guests often walk down to the 12th century Crown hotel in the village. The large front bedroom enjoys a new, old-fashioned bathroom with a claw-foot tub. The spacious blue twin and a third bedroom share a large immaculate bathroom. Chiddingfold is conveniently located 40 miles from both Gatwick and Heathrow airports. Guests often visit Petworth house, Bignor Roman villa, Chichester, Portsmouth and the south coast. *Directions:* From Guildford take the A3 and the A283 to Chiddingfold. Pickhurst Road is off the green and Greenaway is the third house on the right with the large dovecote in front.

GREENAWAY
Owners: Sheila and John Marsh
Pickhurst Road
Chiddingfold
Surrey GU8 4TS
tel: (01428) 682920 fax: (01428) 685078
3 rooms, 1 with private bathroom
From £27.50 per person
Closed Christmas
Children welcome

Ashen Clough, Isobel and Norman Salisbury's home, began life in the 16th century as a prosperous yeoman's home set in a rural Derbyshire valley. Norman was for many years the local vet then retired to take on domestic duties helping Isobel run their lovely home as the most welcoming of Wolsey Lodges. Guests dine with their hosts around the ancient refectory table in the low-beamed dining room. Drinks in the comfortable drawing room precede dinner and it is here that guests enjoy coffee and evening-long conversation before retiring to their delightful bedrooms. On Sunday evenings, Norman and Isobel excuse themselves as host and hostess and a sumptuous buffet is provided. Country lanes lead to main roads that quickly transport you to Georgian Buxton with its restored Opera House, Bakewell with its shops and Monday market, the Potteries where you can visit the Royal Crown Derby factories and factory shops, and the great houses of Chatsworth, Haddon, Keddleston and Lyme Hall. *Directions:* From Buxton take the A6 (Manchester road) for 6 miles and at the roundabout turn left at the signpost for Chinley. Follow the B6062 into the village where you turn right and then right again into Maynestone Road. Ashen Clough is on your left after 1¼ miles.

ASHEN CLOUGH   **NEW**
Owners: Isobel and Norman Salisbury
Maynestone Road
Chinley
Derbyshire SK12 6AH
tel: (01663) 750311
3 rooms with private bathrooms
From £28 per person
Open all year
Children over 16
Wolsey Lodge

If you want to stay in a 600-year-old cottage at the heart of an idylically pretty Cotswold town, you can do no better than Rosary Cottage, Rosemary Spencer's home in the center of Chipping Campden's High Street. However, be aware that this is one of the most popular Cotswold towns and parking in the daytime can be problematic. In the evening the tourists depart and the cottage-lined streets are yours to enjoy. Inside, Rosary Cottage is all exposed beams, low doorways, and sloping floors. Up the narrow stairs, the snug bedrooms are beautifully decorated and each has either a tiny ensuite shower room or its bathroom just outside the door—all are quite unsuitable for large suitcases. Rosemary encourages friendly conversation round the breakfast table and provides her guests with a bountiful repast—she used to be the breakfast cook at the Lords of the Manor hotel. Chipping Campden has an ancient Market Hall where sheep from the surrounding farms were sold, and there are lots of interesting little shops, two old churches, and a wide variety of restaurants, bistros, and pubs. A short distance away lies Hidcote, a series of alluring gardens each bordered by sculptured hedges and linked with paths and terraces. Next door, Kiftsgate has exquisite displays of roses. *Directions:* From Broadway take the A44, towards Stow on the Wold, up the hill and turn left for Chipping Campden. At the T-junction turn right into High Street and Rosary Cottage is on your left in the middle of the road.

ROSARY COTTAGE   **NEW**
Owner: Rosemary Spencer
Chipping Campden
Gloucestershire GL55 6AL
tel: (01386) 841145
3 rooms with private bathrooms
From £20 per person
Open all year
Children over 3

Oakfield is the elegant, early-Victorian home of Patricia and Peter Johnson King, a home where standards surpass those of many country house hotels. Decorated in soft pinks and blue-grays, the enormous drawing room is warm and welcoming on even the dullest of days, its tall windows overlooking a broad sweep of lawns. Past the grand piano and up the elegant staircase are three lovely bedrooms. Elizabeth's Room has a half-tester bed softly draped in pale cream and turquoise with a huge, clawfoot tub in the bathroom; Rose is a mass of pink and soft-blue cabbage roses; and Chinese is smartly Oriental with peach watered-silk wallpaper and a black satin bedspread coordinating with peach and black draperies. With advance notice Patricia is happy to cook a four-course dinner where she and Peter dine with their guests. Otherwise, guests often walk to Highways Haunt in the village. A full-size billiard room is there for you to use as is a large heated swimming pool. The gardens contain an unusual Victorian fern garden. Oakfield is ideally situated for exploring Dartmoor National Park, the cathedral city of Exeter, and the south Devon coast. *Directions:* From Exeter take the A38 towards Plymouth for 8 miles. Turn left for Chudleigh and after 1 mile Oakfield is on your right before you come to the center of the village.

OAKFIELD
Owners: Patricia and Peter Johnson King
Chudleigh
Devon TQ13 0DD
tel: (01626) 852194 fax: (01626) 852194
3 rooms with private bathrooms
From £30 per person
Open all year
Children over 12
Wolsey Lodge

This pretty village of flint-walled, tile-roofed cottages is no longer "next the sea," but separated from it by a vast saltwater marsh formed as the sea retreated. The massive structure of Cley Mill stands as a handsome monument to man's ability to harness the forces of nature. Guests enter the Mill directly into the beamed dining room decorated with country-style pine furniture. The circular sitting room has large chintz chairs drawn round a stone fireplace whose mantle is a sturdy beam displaying toby jugs. Stacked above the sitting room are two large circular bedrooms with ensuite bathrooms: the Wheat Chamber is where the grain was stored and the Stone Room is where the massive grinding stones crushed the flour. Two additional small bedrooms share a bathroom. During the day the mill is open to the public to visit the observation room and the wooden cap of the mill with its massive gears and complex mechanisms that once turned the grinding stones. The old boathouse and stables in the yard have been converted into small, self-catering cottages. Birdwatching, sailing, cycling, and walking are popular pastimes in the area. The seaside towns of Sheringham, Cromer, and Wells are close at hand. There are a great many stately homes to explore such as Sandringham House, the Royal Family's country residence, Jacobean Fellbrigg Hall, Holkham, and Blickling Hall. *Directions:* From King's Lynn follow the A149 around the coast to Cley next the Sea, where the windmill is well signposted.

CLEY MILL GUEST HOUSE
Managers Jenny and Tim Mallam
Cley next the Sea
Holt
Norfolk NR25 7NN
tel: (01263) 740209
6 rooms, 4 with private bathrooms
From £25 per person
Closed February
Children over 6

Low Barns near Corbridge is an excellent base for exploring the remains of the Roman Hadrian's Wall, begun in 120 AD to defend the northernmost boundary of the Empire from attack, and for exploring rural Northumberland. Adjoining the farmhouse a barn has been cleverly converted into comfortable guest accommodation where the rooms have exposed stone walls, beams, low, deeply-set little windows with views of the countryside, and attractive furnishings with comfortable chairs for reading or watching television. The upstairs rooms are more spacious, though the ground floor bedroom is appreciated by guests who have difficulty with stairs. Two additional bedrooms share a bathroom. Breakfast and dinner are served on the large pine table in the farmhouse kitchen and most of the vegetables come from Tom's well-tended vegetable plot. If you have been on the road for a while Sue will allow you to do a load of laundry. A large map of Northumberland is illustrated with postcards of the county's attractions, showing that Low Barns is a perfect base for exploring the historic towns of Corbridge, Hexham, and Durham and taking a day trip that will take you up the Northumbrian coast to Holy Island. Along the wall Housesteads is the most impressive of the remaining forts. *Directions:* From Newcastle take the A69 (Hexham road) then the B6530 towards Corbridge. Low Barns' driveway is on your right after 1 mile.

LOW BARNS
Owners: Sue and Tom Jones
Thornbrough
Corbridge
Northumberland NE45 5LX
tel: (01434) 632408
5 rooms, 3 with private bathrooms
From £18 per person
Open all year
Credit cards: EC, MC, VS
Children welcome

Just steps from the clifftops on an isolated stretch of Cornish coast, this 16th-century farmhouse snuggles in a hollow round a cobbled courtyard. The polished flagstone floors lead you into the comfortable sitting room with high-backed sofas grouped round the log-burning stove. Guests dine at separate tables and Janet Crocker offers a hearty dinner with a choice of starter, main course, and dessert. Farmhouse bedrooms range from small to spacious. If you are a party of four, opt for the more spacious contemporary accommodation offered by nearby Samphire House. Here you enjoy two double bedrooms and a large sitting room with a balcony which overlooks a sheltered swimming pool. It's very much a family operation where Janet runs the farmhouse, while her husband, four sons and their wives manage the farm, tearoom, and self-catering cottages. A visitors' center emphasizes the preservation of this lovely coastline. The clifftops offer magnificent views and a path leads to Strangles Beach where Thomas Hardy loved to walk with his first wife Emma. Walking the coastal path and the nearby villages of Boscastle and Tintagel are great attractions. *Directions:* From Bude, take the A39 towards Camelford and then turn right to Crackington Haven. At the beach, take the right-hand turn at the bottom of the hill for Trevigue and you find Trevigue Farm atop the cliffs after 2 miles.

TREVIGUE FARM   **NEW**
Owners: Janet and Ken Crocker and family
Crackington Haven
Bude
Cornwall EX23 0LQ
tel: (01840) 230418
5 rooms with private bathrooms
From £19 per person
Open March to October
Children over 12

This picture-book farmhouse surrounded by a pretty garden and apple orchards is idyllic and just a two-minute drive from the attractive town of Cranbrook with its white board houses and shops, medieval church, and huge, white board windmill with enormous sails. Guests have a large sitting/dining room with comfy chairs set before an enormous inglenook fireplace and a dining table for breakfast and dinner. The large downstairs bedroom has views to the garden, and an ensuite shower room, and is large enough to accommodate an extra bed. Up a broad flight of creaking stairs is a glorious four-poster room where sunny yellow fabrics complement the dark woods of the floor and bed. The third bedroom has a small sitting room and ensuite bathroom and is prettily decorated with Laura Ashley fabrics. Sissinghurst Castle with its lovely garden is nearby and Bridget and Robin find that guests often visit Canterbury and its famous cathedral—they encourage them to time their visit to include choral evensong. The local vineyards and old railway at Tenterden are other popular attractions. *Directions:* Take the A21 south from Sevenoaks, turn left at the A262 before Lamberhurst and right onto the A229. Go into Cranbrook and take a sharp left after the school. Tilsden Lane (not marked) is the third right, and Hancocks' driveway is the first track on the left.

HANCOCKS FARMHOUSE
Owners: Bridget and Robin Oaten
Tilsden Lane
Cranbrook
Kent TN17 3PH
tel: (01580) 714645
3 rooms with private bathrooms
From £22.50 per person
Open all year
Children over 9

Everything about The Old Cloth Hall is exceptional, from the vast expanses of gardens with manicured lawns, roses, rhododendrons, and azaleas to the dignified old house, parts of which date back more than 500 years. Settle into the richly paneled drawing room with its commodious sofas and chairs drawn round the crackling log fire that blazes in the enormous inglenook. The Old Cloth Hall has been Katherine Morgan's home for many years and because it is a large house she has an array of bedrooms that can be used for guest accommodation which she prices by size and location. If you are on a stringent budget request the small downstairs twin. If you want to splurge ask for The Four Poster room and you will receive a king-size, four-poster decked and draped in lemon and green sprigged fabric with an enormous bathroom. Elizabeth I came for lunch in 1573 but you can stay for dinner and dine with your fellow guests. Guests are welcome to use the unheated swimming pool and the tennis court. Cranbrook is one hour from London, Dover, Canterbury, and Brighton. Sir Winston Churchill's home, Chartwell, Knole, Igtham Mote, Penshurt Place, and Batemans, Rudyard Kipling's home, are within easy reach. *Directions:* Take the A21 south from Sevenoaks, turn left at the A262 before Lamberhurst and right onto the A229 towards Tenterden. Go into Cranbrook and take a sharp left after the school, follow this road for about a mile, turn right just before the cemetery, and the entrance to The Old Cloth Hall is on your right.

THE OLD CLOTH HALL
Owner: Katherine Morgan
Cranbrook
Kent TN17 3NR
tel: (01580) 712220
3 rooms with private bathrooms
From £70 double
Open all year
Children by arrangement
Wolsey Lodge

Before moving to Halfway House, Belle and Peter Hepworth and their four children lived at Crayke castle in the village. Belle and Peter welcome guests as they would their visiting friends—guests do become friends, with a great many of them returning to this pretty part of Yorkshire. Guests have added their contributions to the collection of sugar tongs in the lovely drawing room where you gather for drinks, before enjoying a candlelit dinner round the refectory table in the paneled dining room (the paneling comes from a Jacobean manor house). One lovely, twin-bedded bedroom is found in the house. For complete privacy, opt for the stableyard rooms. Downstairs a beautiful four-poster bed just fits beneath the ceiling beams, while upstairs the beamed hayloft is decorated with blue stocks on the draperies and bedspread. Belle has gone to great lengths to see that bedrooms, and bathrooms are carefully color-coordinated right down to matching china for the tea and coffee trays and information folders. Castle Howard is just a short drive away, while York with its minster and plethora of sightseeing lies 12 miles south. The lovely North Yorkshire Moors and Captain Cook country are yours to explore. *Directions:* From York, take the A19 towards Thirsk for 12 miles to Easingwold, where you turn right for Crayke. Go through the market place and after 1 mile Halfway House is on your right.

HALFWAY HOUSE **NEW**
Owners: Belle and Peter Hepworth
Crayke
York YO6 4TJ
tel: (01347) 822614 fax: (01347) 822942
3 rooms with private bathrooms
From £30 per person
Closed Christmas
Credit cards: EC, MC, VS
Children over 12
Wolsey Lodge

When you stay at The Old Manor, you get far more than bed-and-breakfast in a 16th-century house—you can tour its motor museum, make friends with the army of ducks and geese that wander around the yard, and visit the contented, muddy pigs who wallow at the bottom of the garden. Inside there are cozy beamed rooms and the gentle ticking of Liz and John's clock collection. Books line the walls of the breakfast room and guests eat together round the trestle table before a log fire. The small yellow sitting room at the top of the stairs is for guests to use. A large double bedroom has a snug, ensuite shower room while the two twin rooms share a bathroom down the hallway. Liz is very aware that guests always enjoy their own bathroom facilities, so she rents only one of the twin bedrooms at a time. John is happy to show you his transportation collection which includes an AC Cobra, a 1910 AC Sociable and a 1934 Aston Martin. Warwick Castle, Coventry, and a multitude of Cotswold villages are within half an hour's drive. The Oxford Canal runs along the bottom of the garden and you can walk for miles along its towpath. *Directions:* Exit the M40 at junction 11 (Banbury) and take the A361 towards Daventry for 2½ miles, turn left to Cropredy, cross the canal, turn left at the T-junction, and The Old Manor is on your left.

THE OLD MANOR   **NEW**
Owners: Liz and John Atkins
Cropredy, Banbury
Oxfordshire OX17 1PS
tel: (01295) 750235 fax: (01295) 758479
3 rooms, 2 with private bathrooms
From £22 per person
Closed Christmas and New Year
Credit cards: all major
Children welcome
No Smoking house

Fulford House is one of those interesting homes that has evolved over the years. The earliest parts date back to the 1600s with various bits added from time to time—hence the interesting way you step up and down as you go from room to room. Guests are welcomed as visiting friends and encouraged to make themselves at home in the comfortable sitting room with its slipcovered chairs and soft peach walls. Dinner is house-party style with other guests round the large circular dining-room table. Marypen and Stephen dine with their guests only when just one couple is dining. Blowzy roses decorate the curtains and bed ruffles of the largest bedroom whose ensuite bathroom is up a short flight of stairs. For families a large twin room and a small single can share a bathroom across the hall. A booklet in each bedroom gives an in-depth history of Culworth and suggests enough sightseeing excursions to keep you busy for a week including Sulgrave Manor, George Washington's ancestral home, Warwick Castle, Stratford upon Avon, Coventry cathedral, exquisite Hidcote Manor gardens and Fulford House's own acre of delightful gardens which Marypen and Stephen are justifiably very proud of. *Directions:* From the M40 junction 11 roundabout take the A422 towards Brackley, after 1 mile take B4525 signposted Northampton. After 2 miles turn left to Culworth. Turn right alongside the village green and Fulford House is on your left.

FULFORD HOUSE
Owners: Marypen and Stephen Wills
Culworth
Banbury
Oxon OX17 2BB
tel: (01295) 760355 fax: (01295) 768304
3 rooms, 2 with private bathrooms
From £22 per person
Open mid-February to mid-November
Children over 5
Wolsey Lodge

With its medieval, beamed barn, creeper-covered farmhouse, and flower-filled courtyard, Hillards presents an inviting picture. Owners Jeannie Wilkins and Mike Carter and their four cats occupy a small cottage to one side of the courtyard, giving the entire farmhouse over to guests who enjoy both a television room and a comfortable lounge for relaxing. The rooms tend to be on the dark side: dark wooden furniture, dark fabrics, small windows, dark oak paneling, and exposed, gray stone walls do not give a light and airy feel to the house. While I enjoyed the Jacuzzi tub in the master bedroom, the courtyard room with its little window seats was a special favorite. Mike is busy converting outbuildings into suites with a bedroom and a living room. Breakfast is the only meal served, though plans are under way to convert the ancient barn into a restaurant. Strung out along a busy road, Curry Rivel village is not a tourist destination but Jeannie will outline a driving tour that quickly has you deep in pretty countryside visiting her favorite willow basket producers. Wells with its gorgeous cathedral and Glastonbury steeped in Arthurian legend are popular places to visit. *Directions:* Leave the M25 motorway at junction 25, taking the A358 towards Chard to the A378 to Curry Rivel. Hillards is on your left as you enter the village.

HILLARDS
Owners: Jeannie Wilkins and Mike Carter
High Street
Curry Rivel
Langport
Somerset TA10 0EY
tel: (01458) 251737 fax: (01458) 253233
10 rooms with private bathrooms
From £27.50 per person
Open all year
Children over 12

Ford House is a three-story, Regency-style home which was built for the owner of one of the many shipyards that flourished in Dartmouth during the 19th century. Owner Dick Turner's Australian easy, laid-back manner is echoed in his partner Henri (Henrietta) Firth. Guests go upstairs and downstairs to their bedrooms from the combination sitting and dining room. Garden-level bedrooms are confusingly called the King Room (it has an American queen-sized bed) and the Twin Room, which, more often than not, has its twin beds zipped together as a king. Upstairs you find Tony's Room, where old sewing machines decorate the top of the armoire and the bed is placed at an angle to capture the view across the rooftops of the town. While there are lots of restaurants in town, Henri is happy, with advance notice, to provide an evening meal if guests do not want to go out again after a long day's sightseeing. A fun day trip involves taking a ferry and steam train into Paignton. On Tuesdays, in summer, you can take the ferry to Totnes and stroll around the market admiring the townsfolk in their colorful Elizabethan costumes. *Directions:* From Totnes, take the A381 to Halwell and the A3122 to Dartmouth, where you take the first feeder lane to the right into Townstal Road, which becomes Victoria Road. If you go down a long straight hill you've gone too far.

FORD HOUSE   **NEW**
Owners: Henri Firth and Dick Turner
44 Victoria Road
Dartmouth
Devon TQ6 9DX
tel: (01803) 834047
3 rooms with private bathrooms
From £30 per person
Open March to December
Credit cards: EC, MC, VS
Children welcome

When Rosalie and Ian Buckle first moved to Dunsley Hall, once a wealthy shipping family's grand holiday home, it was in a badly neglected state. The Buckles set to work exposing the oak floor, refurbishing the golden oak paneling, adding modern bathrooms, and turning part of the hall into four self-catering units. Then they relandscaped the gardens, tidied up the tennis courts, and built a spectacular indoor heated pool and fitness room. The piece de resistance of this lovely home is the large billiard room which has golden oak-paneled walls, a massive carved fireplace with built-in seats, and beautiful stained glass windows depicting square-riggers sailing on an aqua sea beneath a cloud-dappled sky. The paneled lounge is snug and cozy with its old-fashioned fireplace and soft carpet. The bedrooms are beautifully decorated in pastel-colored wallpapers with coordinating drapes framing the stone-mullioned windows. A large downstairs corner room has a romantic brass four-poster bed. The nearby North Yorkshire moors with their picturesque villages snuggled into sheltered valleys are a great draw for visitors as are the quaint fishing villages of Runswick Bay, Staithes, and Robin Hood's Bay. *Directions:* From York take the A64 to the A169 Pickering/Whitby road. Cross the moors through Sleights to the A171. Turn left (away from Whitby) and first right to Dunsley. The Hall is in the village on the right.

DUNSLEY HALL
Owners: Rosalie and Ian Buckle
Dunsley
Whitby
Yorkshire YO21 3TL
tel: (01947) 893437 fax: (01947) 893505
7 rooms with private bathrooms
From £36.50 per person
Closed Christmas
Credit cards: all major
Children welcome

Dunster, with its adorable main street dominated by the battlements and towers of Dunster Castle, is a picture-postcard village. Dollons House, once a pharmacy whose chemist also made marmalade for the Houses of Parliament, is a gift shop of English crafts and silk flowers where proprietor Humphrey Bradshaw makes his marmalade for his family and bed and breakfast guests. Up the narrow cottage stairs guests have a cozy sitting room that leads to a patio and pocket-sized garden. Hannah Bradshaw has taken a great deal of care decorating her very pretty bedrooms. Teddy, as the name implies, has cute bears embroidered on its towels and pillows and a whimsical honey bear mural decorating the tiny shower room. Tulips is soft and country in pale pinks with hand-painted tulips on the fabric border that edges the room. Kate's at the back of the house is delightfully white and frilly with a large bathroom and shower. Dunster Castle is open to the public and you can tour 18th-century Dunster Watermill. *Directions:* From Bridgwater take the A39 almost to Minehead. Turn left on the A396 into Dunster, and Dollons is on your right. Pull over outside to unload then park in the High Street or behind the church.

DOLLONS HOUSE
Owner: Hannah and Humphrey Bradshaw
Church Street
Dunster
Minehead
Somerset TA24 6SH
tel: (01643) 821880
3 rooms with private bathrooms
From £22.50 per person
Open all year
Credit cards: EC, MC, VS
Children over 15
No Smoking house

Drakestone House is an exceptional Cotswold-style home filled with an abundance of lovely antiques. The well kept grounds invite a leisurely stroll between the tall, clipped hedges laid out by Hugh's grandfather. The interior of Drakestone House has lovely old pine pitch and narrow wood floors and beamed and plasterwork ceilings, complemented by traditional firebaskets filled with dried flower arrangements and beautiful old furniture. Guests enjoy breakfast round the dining room table where Crystal will, with advance arrangements, also serve dinner for guests' first evening's stay. Upstairs, two bedrooms share the facilities of a large, old-fashioned bathroom which has been modernized. There is also a suite which has an adjoining private bath, a small twin-bedded room suitable for children (crib available), and a larger, double-bedded room that has windows with views both to the side and the front of the house. From Drakestone House you can visit Berkeley Castle and the adjacent Jenner Museum, Slimbridge Wildfowl Trust, Westonbirt Arboretum, and, farther afield, Gloucester, Cheltenham, Bath, and Bristol. *Directions:* Northbound travelers leave the M5 at exit 14; southbound at exit 13. Stinchcombe is situated halfway between Dursley and Wotton-under-Edge on the B4060. Drakestone House is signposted on the road.

DRAKESTONE HOUSE
Owners: Crystal and Hugh St John Mildmay
Stinchcombe
Dursley
Gloucestershire GL11 6AS
tel: (01453) 542140
3 rooms, 1 with private bathroom
From £23 per person
Open April to mid-October
Children welcome
No Smoking house
Wolsey Lodge

Ronald is the keenest of gardeners and his acres of grounds are a delight: plant filled borders line the tumbling stream, the herbaceous border is ablaze with summer flowers, and the water meadow offers some unusual plant species. Jackie loves to share her beautiful home with guests who can choose from three very different bedrooms. The Cottage Suite offers a low-ceilinged bedroom, snug sitting room with television and VCR with sofas which can be made into extra beds, and a small bathroom. In contrast, the Master Suite offers a large high-ceilinged room with a queen-sized bed, television and VCR, and a large, luxurious Victorian-style bathroom. The Pine Bedroom takes its name from the enormous pine-fitted cupboard that has been there since the house was built: its bathroom is down the hall (plans are afoot to make it ensuite). You are welcome to bring your own wine to accompany dinner. If you prefer to eat out, the Foresters Arms is just a two-minute walk away. There are eight classic gardens in South Somerset. Wells and Glastonbury are within easy touring distance as is the Dorset Coast. *Directions:* From Yeovil, take the A30 (Crewkerne road) for 2 miles to the Yeovil Court Hotel. Turn immediately left at the signpost for East Coker, North Coker, and Hardington. Pass the Foresters Arms, and Holywell House is the next driveway on the right.

HOLYWELL HOUSE   **NEW**
Owners: Jackie and Ronald Somerville
Holywell
East Coker
Yeovil
Somerset BA22 9NQ
tel: (01935) 862612 fax: (01935) 863035
3 rooms with private bathrooms
From £25 per person
Closed Christmas
Children welcome

Anthony's forbears have farmed hereabouts for over 300 years and he continues in the family tradition. When Anthony and Alison married they knocked two small cottages into one and added on to the rear to form a spacious home with gardens terracing down to fields and the most spectacular view across the sky-wide fens to Ely Cathedral, a building so large that it dwarfs the little market town that surrounds it. This captivating vista is enjoyed by the very spacious guest bedrooms which occupy wings at either end of the house. At night the cathedral is floodlit and presents a spectacular sight. The bedrooms are light and fresh, with white walls, flowered drapes, pretty bedspreads, and immaculate ensuite bathrooms. Breakfast is the only meal served round the lovely old dining-room table in the beamed dining room and guests often dine at The Anchor in Sutton Gault or The Fire Engine House in Ely which serves traditional Fenland food such as smoked eel and pheasant. Cambridge, whose university complex spans over 700 years of history, is a big draw for visitors who stroll through its college courtyards, explore its ancient alleys, and punt or row under the willow trees that line the River Cam. Among Ely's narrow streets are the house where Cromwell lived, Goldsmith's tower and museum, and the enormous cathedral built in 1083. *Directions:* Take the A10 from Cambridge to Ely, approximately 14 miles, turn right at the roundabout onto the A142 towards Newmarket, and Stuntney is on your right. Lower Road is opposite the church.

FORGE COTTAGE
Owners: Alison and Anthony Morbey
Lower Road
Stuntney, Ely
Cambridgeshire CB7 5TN
tel: (01353) 663275 fax: (01353) 662260
2 rooms with private bathrooms
From £22.50 per person
Closed Christmas
Children over 10

Julie Graham provides a sincere and relaxed welcome to Ettington Manor and is happy to show guests around her home which has greatly evolved since its original portion was built as a religious establishment in 1276. The drawing room has the comfiest of feather sofas drawn up around an enormous log-burning fireplace. In the adjacent dining room Julie serves dinner by prior arrangement at 7:30 pm, or a pre-theater supper at 6:00 pm. Three bedrooms are attractively furnished with new pine furniture and each has a modern, ensuite shower room. The fourth is particularly dramatic with a four-poster bed sitting center stage beneath a high-beamed ceiling, and a snug window seat curving round a stone-mullioned window. Ettington Manor is just five miles from Stratford-upon-Avon and 10 miles from Warwick Castle. Ragley Hall, Kenilworth, the Cotswolds, and an abundance of National Trust properties are nearby. *Directions:* Ettington is on the A422 Banbury to Stratford-upon-Avon road. At the center of the village turn south into Rogers Lane and Ettington Manor is the first driveway on your right.

ETTINGTON MANOR
Owner: Julie Graham
Ettington
Stratford-upon-Avon
Warwickshire CV37 7SX
tel and fax: (01789) 740216
4 rooms with private bathrooms
From £30 per person
Open March to November
Credit cards: EC, MC, VS
Children over 12
No Smoking house
Wolsey Lodge

Over 500 years ago this tiny cottage in this quiet Cotswold village was home to the parish priest and today is a welcoming bed and breakfast. The front door opens into the large guest sitting room where a lovely Welsh dresser holds an array of unusual green and white china and the breakfast room whose massive inglenook fireplace is decorated with country knickknacks. An old lamp hangs over a large round table where guests gather for breakfast, which consists of their choice of traditional bacon and eggs or smoked haddock and kippers. The free-range eggs come from the farm next door and honey from Jan's bees. The three guest bedrooms found at the top of the narrow stairs have lots of simple country charm and each has its own bathroom. A double room has old pine furniture while the large twin has roses peeking in at the window and a view across the fields. Husband David, a banker mason, has carved new stone mullioned windows for the cottage. Exploring the Cotswolds with their rolling hills and pretty villages is most enjoyable but guests also love shopping for clothes and antiques, visiting gardens such as those at Kiftsgate and Hidcote, touring stately homes, and petting the animals in the Cotswold Wildlife Park. *Directions:* Take the Cotswold villages of Chipping Norton, Stow-on-the-Wold and Moreton in Marsh as a triangle on the map and the small village of Evenlode is at the center of the triangle. Twostones is next to the church.

TWOSTONES
Owners: Jan and David Wright
Evenlode
Moreton in Marsh
Gloucestershire GL56 0NY
tel: (01608) 51104
3 rooms with private bathrooms
From £18 per person
Open all year
Children over 10

Hyde Farm House was once the principal farm on the Frampton estate. When the estate was sold Frampton Manor was transported stone-by-stone to America and the farmhouse fell upon sad times to be rescued by John and Jan who took five years to restore it to the glorious home you see today. The minimum of regimentation is the order of the day so guests can dine at the time of their choosing and while John cooks, Jan (he hails from Norway) looks after guests seating them either at the long table in the dining room or in the conservatory overlooking the garden. Guests are encouraged to bring their own wine. Strains of classical music accompany dinner and coffee in the most inviting of drawing rooms. Staffordshire flatback figures (Napoleon, Dick Whittington and Queen Victoria amongst them) line the staircase which leads to the delightful bedrooms. Chatsworth is a particularly elegant room with its draped bed and large bathroom. This rural corner of Dorset is Thomas Hardy country set between Maiden Newton (Chalk Newton) and Frampton (Scrimpton) and just 7 miles from the sea at Abbotsbury. It is an easy drive to over 20 gardens and 15 National Trust properties. Bring your rod and enjoy Hyde Farm House's private fishing. *Directions:* Take the A37 from Dorchester towards Yeovil for 5 miles and turn left on the A356 (Crewkerne road) into Frampton. Pass the church on your right, the village hall your left and Hyde Farm House is on your left after 500 yards.

HYDE FARM HOUSE   **NEW**
Owners: John Saunders and Jan Faye-Schjoll
Dorchester Road
Frampton
nr Dorchester
Dorset DT2 9NG
tel: (01300) 320272
3 rooms with private bathrooms
From £25 per person
Open all year
Children over 12

When Mary and Tony Dakin bought The Old Parsonage at an auction, it was in a sad state of disrepair and they have put a great deal of work into making it the lovely home you see today. In the days when clerics were men of substance, there were six servants for the house and garden, but now its just Mary, Tony, and the tractor mower. In the morning, Tony cooks breakfast while Mary takes their young sons to school. Typical of grand Georgian houses, the rooms are tall and spacious and the Dakins have furnished them in a most delightful manner. Unfortunately, I was unable to see the bedrooms, but photos show them to be as attractive as the delightfully furnished public rooms. Tony is a keen gardener and the sunny conservatory is always full of plants. He is also passionate about photography and has framed photos of longtime village residents lining the hallway. Frant is a most attractive village set round a green, with two pubs and a restaurant, Bassetts, where guests usually go for dinner. There are fifteen houses, castles, and gardens to visit in the area, amongst them Leeds, Scotney, Bodiam, Sissinghurst, and Hever Castles. London is a 40-minute train ride from Frant station. *Directions:* From Tunbridge Wells, take the A267 south for 2½ miles to Frant. Turn left at the 30mph Frant sign, and The Old Parsonage is on your left, just before the church.

THE OLD PARSONAGE   **NEW**
Owners: Mary and Tony Dakin
Church Lane
Frant
Tunbridge Wells
Kent TN3 9DX
tel and fax: (01892) 750773
3 rooms with private bathrooms
From £27.50 per person
Open all year
Credit cards: all major
Children welcome

The soothing sound of water splashing down the mill race is the only sound that breaks the countryside peace and quiet when staying at Maplehurst Mill, the site of a mill since 1309. Heather feels that eating here is an integral part of the stay and guests dine by candlelight in the ancient miller's house with its beams and inglenook fireplace. Bottomend, a ground-floor bedroom, sits directly above the mill race and its windows open onto the moss-covered millwheel. Topend, at the top of the mill, has a beamed bathroom and the four-poster room which overlooks the meadows has its bed strategically placed on the sloping floor. The room across the garden in the stables lacks the warm country character of those in the mill. A heated swimming pool overlooks the fields. Idencroft Herb Gardens are just round the corner and Brattle Farm, an old-fashioned working farm, is an excellent choice for those who have visited all Kent's castles, gardens, and stately homes. *Directions:* From the M20 take the A229 Hastings exit and follow Hastings signs through Maidstone for 12 miles to Staplehurst. At the end of the village turn left into the Frittenden road. After 1¼ miles, opposite a white house, turn right into a narrow lane. At the end turn right and the mill is at the foot of the incline.

MAPLEHURST MILL
Owners: Heather and Kenneth Parker
Mill Lane
Frittenden
Kent TN17 2DT
tel: (01580) 852203
5 rooms with private bathrooms
From £28 per person
Open all year
Credit cards: EC, MC, VS
Children over 12
No Smoking house
Wolsey Lodge

Goldhill Mill (mentioned in the Domesday Book of 1086) was a working mill for over 800 years. The mill wheel still turns behind a glass partition in the kitchen where Shirley chats to guests as she cooks them breakfast. After breakfast, feed your toast to the swans who reside on the millpond. The Coles have compiled a list of recommended restaurants and pubs for dinner, including comments and prices. Two of Shirley's great-great-grandfather's paintings of Egypt hang in the comfortable guests' sitting room—he was the artist on Carter's 1922 expedition which discovered Tutankhamen's tomb. Unlike so many expedition members, he did not succumb to the "curse" and lived into old age—part of which was spent in this house. The bedrooms are very luxurious. Pink has a romantic pastel decor and luxurious bathroom with Jacuzzi tub. Millpool overlooks the millpool and is all lilacs and roses on the wallpaper, drapes, and bedspread. The Four-Poster room overlooks acres of garden towards the tennis court. Across the courtyard are two deluxe self-catering cottages that sleep 4 to 6 persons. Kent abounds in castles, and stately homes. *Directions:* From Tonbridge, take the A26 (signposted Maidstone) for 2 miles. Turn right down Three Elm Lane, and after 1¼ miles left into the mill's driveway.

GOLDHILL MILL   **NEW**
Owners: Shirley and Vernon Cole
Golden Green
Tonbridge
Kent TN11 0BA
tel: (01732) 851626 fax: (01732) 851881
3 rooms with private bathrooms
From £33.75 per person
Closed mid-July to September
Credit cards: EC, MC, VS
Children over 16
No Smoking house

Set in acres of lovely gardens which include a grass tennis court and heated swimming pool, Ennys is an idyllic, 17th-century manor house set deep in Cornish countryside, three miles from St Michael's Mount. Polished flagstones line the hallway leading to the garden where on a summer evening guests gather at 7:00 pm for a chat over sherry before going in to dinner where four little dining tables are set around the fireplace. On cool evenings, drinks are served in the cheery sitting room. Upstairs are three lovely bedrooms, two of them delectable four-posters. Families are welcome in the suites which occupy an adjacent barn—bedrooms here are also delightfully appointed, though without the bric-a-brac that children find so hazardous. St Michael's Mount is a "must do," as is spending an evening at the open-air Minack theater in Porthcurno. A delightful day trip involves an hour's countryside walk (or a short drive) to the railway station where you take a train to St Ives to visit the Tate Gallery which displays the work of 20th-century St Ives artists. *Directions:* From Exeter, take the A30 to Crowlas village which is 4 miles before Penzance. Turn towards Helston, at the roundabout, and at the next roundabout turn left at the signpost for Relubbus. Go through Goldsithney to St Hilary, and when the Ennys Farm's signpost is on the right, turn left and follow the lane for a mile to the farm.

ENNYS FARM **NEW**
Owners: Susan and John White
St Hilary, Goldsithney
Penzance
Cornwall TR20 9BZ
tel: (01736) 740262
5 rooms with private bathrooms
From £20 per person
Closed Christmas
Children welcome in family suites

Sitting beside the village green at the heart of this quiet, unspoilt Cotswold village, The Lamb is a picture-perfect hostelry. Locals gather in the evening in the quaint bar where pride of place is given to a picture gallery of guide dogs for the blind who have been sponsored by patrons' donations. Decked out in pine, the restaurant with its soft pink decor is most attractive. The menu is a la carte with such dishes as beef Wellington and grilled lamb cutlets with onion sauce. Simpler fare is served in the bar and adjacent buttery. Up the narrow, winding staircase and down twisting, narrow corridors are an array of cottage-style bedrooms, all furnished differently (suitable only for the nimble of foot). Two have intricately carved four-poster beds made by Richard. Families often take the two twin bedrooms which share a bathroom. Thick stone walls with deeply set windows, low ceilings, quaint doors, and beams all add to the old-world feel. The two rooms in the converted stable are not as attractive. Outside is a landscaped garden—the perfect place to enjoy a glass of real ale on a warm summer evening—and a heated indoor swimming pool. Most people come here to tour the picturesque Cotswold villages, explore gardens such as Hidcote, and visit Stratford-upon-Avon and Oxford. *Directions:* From the A429 turn into Bourton-on-the-Water, carry on this road (not into the village) and take the first turn right to Great Rissington.

THE LAMB INN
Owners: Kate and Richard Cleverly
Great Rissington
Bourton on the Water
Gloucestershire GL54 2LD
tel: (01451) 820388
11 rooms, 9 with private bathrooms
Double from £42 to £72
Closed Christmas
Credit cards: EC, MC, VS
Children welcome

Church House, a spacious, Georgian home, has a sweep of driveway circling to the front door beneath massive copper beeches. To the rear are lawns, sheep pasture, and a helicopter landing pad for those who care to arrive by air. Guests have a high-ceilinged, comfortable, yellow drawing room where Anna displays her collection of paintings by West Country artist Reg Gammon. Anna is happy with advanced notice to prepare dinner. Guests eat together round the long, polished table and you are welcome to bring your own wines. A graceful wooden staircase spirals its way up to the top floor and the homey guest rooms. The largest bedroom has its private bathroom across the hall while the other three rooms have their facilities in the room, artfully concealed behind tall wooden screens. Ask for the one with the view from the loo of Grittleton rooftops. On the landing is an information table showing all the things to do and see in the area, though guests are welcome to spend their days relaxing around the heated swimming pool. Grittleton is well placed to visit Bath, Bristol, Malmesbury, Tetbury, and the picture-perfect village of Castle Combe. Every May the Badminton horse trials are held nearby. *Directions:* Exit the M4 at junction 17, taking the A429 towards Cirencester and almost immediately (at the crossroads) turn left for the 3½ mile drive to Grittleton. Church House is beside the church.

CHURCH HOUSE
Owners: Anna and Michael Moore
Grittleton
Chippenham
Wiltshire SN14 6AP
tel: (01249) 782562   fax: (01249) 782562
4 bedrooms with private bathrooms
From £25 per person
Open all year
Children over 12

Surrounded by a sky-wide landscape of fields, this converted 19th-century oast offers spacious accommodation within a half hour's drive of Kent's most celebrated tourist attractions. The lower half of the roundels, where the hops were roasted, has been converted into a spacious sitting room, but, more often than not, guests gather in the open-plan kitchen that was formerly a barn. If you would like to eat in, Ann discusses the menu at length and precedes the four-course meal with drinks in the sitting room. Two bedrooms (a twin and a double) occupy the upper reaches of the roundels and share a well-equipped bathroom. The third bedroom is very large and has its bathroom ensuite. Sasha, the friendly golden retriever, is a great favorite with guests. Anne gives her guests lists of places to visit and a map of pubs and restaurants in the area to assist them in making sightseeing and dining decisions. Nearby places of interest include Chartwell (Churchill's home), 13th-century Hever Castle, the onetime home of the Boleyn family, and Penshurst Place, a 14th-century manor house. *Directions:* From Tonbridge, take the A26 towards Maidstone. After the village of Hadlow, pass Leavers Manor Hotel on the right and turn right into Stanford Lane. Leavers Oast is the third driveway on your right.

LEAVERS OAST   **NEW**
Owners: Ann and Denis Turner
Stanford Lane
Hadlow
Kent TN11 0JN
tel and fax: (01732) 850924
3 rooms, 1 ensuite
From £27 per person
Open all year
Children over 12
No Smoking house

There are many good reasons to visit Leicestershire and this exceptional home at the edge of a peaceful village with many picturesque thatched cottages is one of them. Here old furniture is gleamingly polished, the windows sparkle, and everything is in apple-pie order. The evening sun streams into the drawing room and books on stately homes and castles invite browsing. Breakfast is served in a small dining room with a long trestle table. If there are several people for dinner, Raili (who grew up in Finland) sets the elegant table in the large dining room and serves a variety of meals using organic vegetables from her garden. The principal bedroom has ensuite facilities, while the other three guestrooms share a large family bathroom. Bedrooms have televisions and someone is always on hand to make a pot of tea. A three-day Christmas program gives guests the opportunity to experience a quiet, traditional English country Christmas— visits to the hunt and the midnight carol service are highlights. Nearby are a great many stately homes (Burghley House, and Rockingham Castle, for instance), lots of antique shops, the vast expanse of Rutland Water, cathedrals at Ely and Peterborough, historic towns (Stamford and Uppingham), and ancient villages. *Directions:* From Uppingham take the A47 and turn left at East Norton for Hallaton. Drive through the village and The Old Rectory is next to the church.

THE OLD RECTORY
Owners: Raili and Tom Fraser
Hallaton
Market Harbourough
Leicestershire LE16 8TY
tel: (0185889) 350
3 rooms, 1 with private bathroom
From £26 per person
Open all year
Children over 7
Wolsey Lodge

Sandbarn Farm was originally part of the Lucy family's estate at nearby Charlecote. During the 1980s this 16th-century farmhouse was extensively modernized and now it is home to Helen and Paul Waterworth who offer guests a quiet countryside retreat just fifteen minutes' drive from Stratford-upon-Avon. Guests have a snug television lounge and eat breakfast together round the dining-room table. A pub in the village serves meals, but Helen is also happy to suggest restaurants in Stratford-upon-Avon. Under the eaves, two large bedrooms can either be twin-bedded or zipped together as king-sized, and each has a spacious bathroom and additional single bedroom (no reduction for children). A third bedroom has its private bathroom across the hallway. The Lucy family have resided across the fields at Charlcote Park since the 1204 in a grand home was extensively modernized during the 19th century. You can tour the Victorian kitchens and grand rooms and enjoy beautiful walks through vast acres of parkland. While Stratford-upon-Avon is a must to visit, also remember to wander into Warwick, with its mixture of Georgian and old timber houses, and it magnificent castle. *Directions:* Exit the M40 at junction 15, and take the A46, Stratford road. At the next roundabout, fork left on the A439 signposted Stratford Town Centre. Turn left at a small crossroads (with a large Mercedes showroom) to Hampton Lucy, and Sandbarn Farm is on the right after 1½ miles.

SANDBARN FARM **NEW**
Owners: Helen and Paul Waterworth
Hampton Lucy
Warwickshire CV35 8AU
tel: (01789) 842280
3 rooms with private bathrooms
From £25 per person
Closed Christmas
Children over 5

No longer a farm, this 17th-century house is the adorable home of Sheila Edwards. Chintz-covered chairs on an Oriental carpet, mullioned windows set into thick walls, blackened beams, an antique dresser displaying china, and an old polished table set before a blazing fire in the inglenook fireplace present the picture of coziness that awaits you at Ford Farm House. Upstairs, guests have a comfortable sitting room with lots of games, a television, tea and coffee tray, and biscuits. The little bedrooms are very pretty: Louise's Room is a sunny single with lots of books, the Patchwork Room has a patchwork quilt on its bed and an ensuite shower room, and the Flower Room has watercolor prints of flowers, a flowery bedspread, and shares a large bathroom with Louise's Room. A delicious breakfast is the only meal served: for dinner guests usually walk up the hill to the nearby Church House Inn. Harberton is well placed for exploring Devon: historic Totnes with its castle, Elizabethan Dartmouth with its naval college, picturesque Salcombe, Buckfastleigh with its abbey, and the wild expanses of Dartmoor National Park. *Directions:* Take the A38 round Exeter, then the A384 to Totnes where you take the A381 Kingsbridge road to your right on the outskirts of town. After 2 miles turn right to Harberton and right at the white cottage and Ford Farm is the next house.

FORD FARM HOUSE
Owner: Sheila Edwards
Harberton
Totnes
Devon TQ9 7SJ
tel: (01803) 863539
3 rooms, 1 with private bathroom
From £19 per person
Open all year
Children over 12

Surrounded by lush green fields, Greenlooms Cottage offers a quiet countryside location just five miles from the heart of medieval Chester. The cottage was the hedger and ditcher's cottage on the Duke of Westminster's Eaton estate. Hezekiah, the last incumbent, lived here for many years with his sister Miriam who raised pigs and geese. Now Greenlooms is home to Deborah and Peter Newman who have sympathetically extended and modernized the cottage, while keeping all its lovely old features, such as the low-beamed ceilings and the pump in the garden. Step through the front door into the old-fashioned pine country kitchen where Deborah serves breakfast. Through the snug television room you come to the cottagey little bedrooms. For dinner, Deborah usually suggests the Grosvenor Arms in Adford or dining in the atmospheric bar at nearby Willington Hall. Rather than looking for parking in the center of Chester, drive to the Park and Ride from where a shuttle bus (runs every ten minutes till 6:00 pm) transports you into town. Conwy Castle and Bodnant Gardens in Wales are a very popular day trip. *Directions:* From Chester take the A41 (Whitchurch road) south for 2 miles, and turn left at Whithouse Antiques (before the Black Dog pub). Follow the road through the village for 1½ miles, turn right into Martins Lane, and Greenlooms Cottage is on your right, after less than a mile.

GREENLOOMS COTTAGE   **NEW**
Owners: Deborah and Peter Newman
Hargrave
Chester
Cheshire CH3 7RY
tel: (01829) 81475
2 rooms with private bathrooms
From £17.50 per person
Open all year
Children welcome

Christine and David Cooper have lovingly and with great imagination converted this mill, barn, and mill house (mentioned in the Domesday Book of 1086) into a secluded hideaway set amid woodland, water, and pasture. In the mill the Dutch-door entrance leads into a sitting room with two round grinding stones on the floor and antique pulleys and gears above. From here separate steep, narrow staircases lead up to two very tiny bedrooms (small suitcases only). Although minute, each bedroom is bright and cheery with sun streaming in from the overhead skylight. The bathrooms are reached by very steep, ladder-like steps down from the bedrooms (definitely not a place to stay for the infirm). The adjacent old wooden barn is all beams and coziness. Downstairs there are a sitting room and small bedroom and up the narrow stairs low doors lead to two additional small bedrooms. The romantic four-poster room's bed is made partially from the timbers of a haywagon. In the double bedroom you have to bend almost double to duck beneath a beam to enter the bathroom. Breakfast is served in the Coopers' mill house. A light supper tray can be ordered. *Directions:* Take the A264 from Tunbridge Wells, then go 1 mile south on the B2026 towards Hartfield. Turn left just past Perryhill Nurseries on the farm track and keep right at the Y.

BOLEBROKE MILL
Owners: Christine and David Cooper
Edenbridge Road
Hartfield
Sussex TN7 4JP
tel: (01892) 770425
4 rooms with private bathrooms
From £27.50 per person
Credit cards: all major
Open March to October
Children over 7
No Smoking house

It was love at first sight when I came upon Carr Head Farm sitting high above Hathersage village with steep crags and windswept heather moors as a backdrop. The garden presents a large flagstone patio, a profusion of flowers nestled in little niches in the terraces leading down to a sweeping lawn, and the most spectacular view across this beautiful Derbyshire valley. The beauty of Mary Bailey's gardens is matched by the loveliness of her home where everything has been done with caring and impeccable taste. The beamed dining room is furnished in period style with groupings of tables and chairs where guests gather for breakfast, the only meal served. The adjacent drawing room is very elegant in blues and creams, a bowl of sweets sitting on the coffee table next to a stack of interesting books. The three lovely bedrooms share the facilities of a bathroom with shower upstairs and another downstairs. The four-poster room offers beautiful views of the valley. The Peak District with its picturesque villages, stone-walled fields, and dramatic dales is on your doorstep, as are Haddon Hall and Chatsworth House. *Directions:* Exit the M1 at junction 29 towards Baslow where you take the A623 to the B6001, through Grindleford to Hathersage. At the junction with the main road, turn right up the village, left into School Lane, and first left. Just before the church (Little John of Robin Hood fame has his grave in the churchyard) turn right up Church Bank to the farm.

CARR HEAD FARM
Owners: Mary and Michael Bailey
Church Bank
Hathersage
Sheffield S30 1BR
tel: (01433) 50383
3 rooms sharing 2 bathrooms
From £17 per person
Closed Christmas
Children over 12

Sheltered in a gentle fold of the hills beneath the spectacular crags of Haytor Rocks, Haytor Vale is a quiet village containing little cottages and The Rock Inn. With its wooden beams and huge open fireplace, the inn has a cozy, traditional ambiance. Bedrooms are named after horses that have won the Grand National: Lovely has an old oak four-poster bed and a dark beamed ceiling, Master Robert and Freebooter are rooms with sloping ceilings and large private bathrooms. A relatively small supplement is charged for these deluxe rooms, and it is well worth paying. All the bedrooms have television (including a movie channel), tea and coffee, telephone, and a mini bar. The food here is delightful: bar meals range from traditional roasts to curries (the desserts are especially tempting), while the candlelit restaurant serves a set-price dinner with a wide variety of choices for each course. From the giant rocky outcrop of neighboring Haytor Rocks you can see the vast extent of Dartmoor National Park, the Teign estuary, and rolling hills of southern Devon. The nearby quarry supplied the stone used for building London Bridge, which now resides in America. *Directions:* Take the M5 from Exeter which joins the A38, Plymouth road, then the A382 to Bovey Tracey. At the first roundabout turn left and follow the road up to Haytor and cross a cattle grid onto the moor. After passing an old petrol station, turn left into Haytor Vale.

THE ROCK INN
Owner: Christopher Graves
Haytor Vale
Newton Abbot
Devon TQ13 9XP
tel: (01364) 661305 fax: (01364) 661242
10 rooms, 8 with private bathrooms
From £27.95 per person
Open all year
Credit cards: all major
Children welcome

Harman is an enthusiastic gardener and loves to host fellow enthusiasts who come to tour the many lovely gardens in Kent. Guests have their own entry which leads to a charmingly furnished, low-beamed sitting room whose walls are lined with interesting books and the brick floor is topped by a pretty rug. In the adjacent dining room, gleaming copper and brass accent the huge inglenook fireplace. Guests dine together, by the soft glow of candlelight, round the polished table. Upstairs, creaking, crooked floors lead to the bedrooms and I particularly admired the spacious Blue Room. The Middle Room's bathroom is next door to it, but plans are afoot to break through the walls, so it may be ensuite by the time you visit. Downstairs, a spacious twin room can accommodate guests who have difficulty walking. Jane has compiled a folder on the many places of interest to visit (you'll need to stay a month if you plan on visiting them all). Another folder covers the plethora of gardens. Amongst the more famous ones are Sissinghurst, Doddington, Mount Ephraim, Pashley Manor, Goodnestone, and Great Dixter. Guests often make day trips to London. *Directions:* Exit the M20 at junction 8 towards Leeds Castle. Go through Leeds village to the A274, turn left and continue through Sutton Valence and one mile beyond Headcorn to the crossroads. Turn right signposted Waterman Quarter and Vine Farm is on the left after ¾ mile.

VINE FARM   **NEW**
Owners: Jane and Tim Harman
Headcorn
Kent TN27 9JJ
tel: (01622) 890203 fax: (01622) 891819
3 rooms with private bathrooms
From £18.50 per person
Open all year
Credit cards: EC, MC, VS
Children over 10
No Smoking house

Cobblestones border the main street of Helperby, a village where the number of shops (four) just outnumbers the pubs. Fronting onto the narrow lane that leads to the church, Brafferton Hall was built in the 1740s as the dower house to the much grander Helperby Hall which lies at the opposite end of the village. Now it is home to Sue and John White who find that their home's spacious, well-proportioned rooms are perfect for entertaining guests country-house style. Sue and John have an easy, friendly manner, so it a pleasure to join them in the garden for pre-dinner drinks, dine with them, and chat afterwards over coffee and chocolates in the drawing room. (Sue thoughtfully feeds children an early supper so that they can be tucked up in bed by dinner time.) If you wish to dine out, the pubs in the village serve food and there are several excellent restaurants within 5 miles. Upstairs the pine room is named after its furniture and has an ensuite shower room. A large twin room and cozy double have their private bathrooms down the hall and a snug little single is perfect for a child. With its central location between the Yorkshire Dales and the Yorkshire Moors, Brafferton Hall is perfectly located for exploring not only the dales and moors, but also Rievaulx and Fountains abbeys, Castle Howard, Shandy Hall, Whitby and the coast, Harrogate, and York. *Directions:* Leave the A1 at Boroughbridge and follow the Easingwold road to Helperby. Take the first turning on the right after the 30 mph sign and Brafferton Hall is on your left after 100 yards.

BRAFFERTON HALL
Owners: Sue and John White
Helperby, York
Yorkshire Y06 2NZ
tel and fax: (01423) 360352
4 rooms with private bathrooms
From £27.50 per person
Open all year
Children welcome
Wolsey Lodge

Hernes has been the Ovey family home for five generations. Surrounded by 400 acres of farmland, this large, rambling home dates from the 16th century with Georgian, Victorian and Edwardian additions and a swimming pool added by Gill and Richard. Guests tend to congregate in the vast billiard room where large sink-in-sofas are gathered round the fireplace, and the coffee table is piled high with books on where to go and what to see. Sometimes it is possible to enjoy a game on the billiards table, but more often it is covered with maps, ready to help guests plan their routes, or as a collecting point for Gillian's current needlepoint project. If you decide to dine out, Gill recommends several traditional pubs in nearby villages. The principal bedroom is a vast four-poster affair with an equally large bathroom that is sometimes warmed by a log burning stove. Two twin-bedded rooms have their bathrooms just across the hallway. When guests have gone to bed, the alarm system is switched on and you are unable to walk downstairs until it is disarmed in the morning. Gill suggests that if guests want to go into London, they drive for 15 minutes to Reading and take the train (45 minutes). The attractive Thameside town of Henley is just a five-minute drive away. *Directions:* From the traffic lights in the center of Henley (not at the bridge) turn south into Duke Street, and first right into Greys Road which winds you to Hernes on your right.

HERNES　　　**NEW**
Owners: Gill and Richard Ovey
Henley on Thames
Oxfordshire RG9 4NT
tel and fax: (01491) 573245
3 rooms with private bathrooms
From £27.50 per person
Open mid-January to mid-December
Children over 2
No Smoking house
Wolsey Lodge

East Peterel Field Farm offers spectacular views of rolling countryside with hardly another building in sight, yet you are just over a mile from the delightful market town of Hexham, and two miles from Hadrian's Wall, the bleak, northernmost outpost of the Roman Empire. The glory of East Peterel Field Farm is its vast country kitchen where guests enjoy breakfast at the long trestle table in front of tall windows which frame the idyllic countryside views. Susan loves to cook, so specials such as salmon cakes and kedgeree are often served at breakfast time (she often gives cookery demonstrations or invites guest chefs to demonstrate their arts). Guests dine together round the dining-room table and are encouraged to bring their own wine to accompany their meal. If she has a large dinner party, Susan serves coffee in the lovely drawing room, but for smaller parties she utilizes the snug, a most attractive room full of comfortable chairs where a log fire bids a cheery welcome. The master bedroom is vast, the twin room lovely, and the small double has its bathroom just next door. David runs a small stud farm where he breeds and raises thoroughbreds—his dream is to breed a Derby winner. Hadrian's Wall is a great attraction hereabouts. The beautiful Northumbrian coast with all its castles is about a 40-mile drive away. *Directions:* From Hexham, turn into Blanchland Road, at the Tap and Spile Pub, bear right at the Y for 1 mile, and take the first farm track to your right after the Black House Restaurant.

EAST PETEREL FIELD FARM   **NEW**
Owners: Susan and David Carr
Hexham
Northumberland NE46 2JT
tel and fax: (01434) 607209
3 rooms with private bathrooms
From £20 per person
Open all year
Children welcome

This timbered, pink house and its black-painted wooden barn hug a quiet country road on the edge of the peaceful Suffolk village of Higham. Meg Parker, with her gentle dalmatian Percy at her heels, offers a warm smile and a sincere welcome to her home, quickly putting visitors at ease. Meg leads her guests to the lovely drawing room and then escorts them up the broad staircase to their rooms. Breakfast is enjoyed around the large dining-room table, and, since it is the only meal served, she is happy to offer advice on where to dine, often suggesting The Angel at Stoke by Nayland. Bedrooms vary in size from large twin-bedded rooms to a cozy double room, in the oldest part of the house, with an ensuite bathroom. Outside, Meg's large garden is carefully tended and stretches towards the River Brett where a punt and a canoe are available for guests' use. The narrow Brett soon becomes the broader Stour and you can punt/paddle upstream for a picnic and idly drift home or go downstream to Stratford St Mary and work off a lunch at The Swan by making your way back upstream. An unheated swimming pool is tucked into one sheltered corner of the garden and a well kept tennis court occupies another. A highlight of a stay here is to visit Flatford, immortalized in the paintings of John Constable. *Directions:* Leave the A12 between Colchester and Ipswich at Stratford St Mary. The Old Vicarage is 1 mile to the west next to the church.

THE OLD VICARAGE
Owners: Meg and John Parker
Higham
Colchester
Suffolk CO7 6JY
tel: (0120) 637248
4 rooms, 2 with private bathrooms
From £24 per person
Open all year
Children welcome
Wolsey Lodge

Pam and Roger Laidler offer a hospitable welcome to their 350-year-old picturebook thatched cottage, Quantock House, nestled in Holford village beneath the Quantock Hills. Breakfast and a good-value-for-money dinner are served in the large beamed sitting and dining room, warmed by a wood-burning stove set in the large inglenook fireplace. Bedrooms are small and cottagey with either a snug, ensuite shower room or a bathroom across the hall. I particularly enjoyed the downstairs bedroom with its little window seat, small shower room, and pine bed topped by a handmade quilt. While everything is quaint and pretty, I found the upstairs bathroom dated in style. Pam loves needlework and there are framed pictures of her and her grandmother's handiwork throughout the house. Coleridge lived in the adjacent village of Nether Stowey when he wrote *The Ancient Mariner*, and guests often tour his cottage. Wordsworth also lived nearby at Alfoxton House which is now a hotel. Nearby Kilve Beach is famous for its fossilized ammonites and the Laidlers have a particularly large one on the back terrace. This is an exceptional walking area and Pam and Roger can suggest pretty walks that last between an hour and a day. *Directions:* From Bridgwater take the A39 (Minehead road) for 12 miles to Holford, where you turn left between the Texaco station and the Plough Inn—Quantock House is on your right.

QUANTOCK HOUSE   **NEW**
Owners: Pam and Roger Laidler
Holford
Bridgwater
Somerset TA5 1RY
tel: (01278) 741439
3 rooms with private bathrooms
From £18 per person
Open all year
Children welcome
No Smoking house

Horsleygate Hall nestles in the sheltered Cordwell valley at the edge of the Peak District National Park. The hall was built in 1783 as a farmhouse and later extended in 1836 and Margaret and Robert have been careful to preserve all its old features such as the old farmhouse kitchen with its blackened Yorkshire range, flagstone floors and the old pine woodwork and doors. Guests have a comfortable, homey sitting room and enjoy breakfast in the adjacent breakfast room. Breakfast is the only meal offered and visitors often eat at the Robin Hood in nearby Holmesfield. The attractively decorated bedrooms overlook the large garden where paths guide you across the lawn and through the different areas which are divided by walls, shrubbery, and fences. I particularly enjoyed the vegetable garden where decorative plantings of vegetables were interspersed with colorful flowers and scented herbs. A grand garden on an infinitely larger scale surrounds Chatsworth House, the enormous home of the Duke and Duchess of Devonshire, full of opulent rooms, priceless paintings, and furniture. Haddon Hall has a fragrant rose garden and a romantic, 14th-century manor house. Bakewell, Ilam, Edensor, Hartington, Ashford-in-the-Water, and Eyam are particularly attractive, villages. *Directions:* Leave the M1 motorway at junction 29 into Chesterfield where you take the B6051 (Hathersage) through Barlow and Millthorpe, then take the first turn right (Horsleygate Lane) and immediately left into Horsleygate Hall's driveway.

HORSLEYGATE HALL
Owners: Margaret and Robert Ford
Horsleygate Lane
Holmesfield, Chesterfield
Derbyshire S18 5WD
tel: (01142) 890333
3 rooms, 1 with private bathroom
From £17 per person
Open all year
Children over 5

The first thing you notice when you come through Woodhayes' front door is the portraits, huge paintings that sometimes stretch from floor to ceiling. Once you have made yourself at home in this friendly house you may be inclined, as I was, to do a "who's who" of Noel's forbears, ascertaining how the congenial pictures in your room are related to all the others. Guests dine by candlelight round the polished dining-room table in what was at one time the home's kitchen—hence the flagstone floors and huge inglenook fireplace which now contains a wood-burning stove. The twin-bedded room at the front of the house has commanding views across the valley while the four-poster room overlooks the rose garden at the side of the house, both have ensuite bathrooms. A single bedroom has its private bathroom down the hall. Dumpdon Celtic hill fort rises behind the house and beyond lies the rolling green of the Blackdown Hills a wonderful place for walking. Nearby Honiton is the historic center for lace making and a small museum chronicles the industry's history and development. A twenty-minute drive brings you to the Victorian resort of Sidmouth and Beer, a fishing village in a little bay. *Directions:* Woodhayes is prominently visible on high ground 1½ miles northeast of Honiton. Take the Dunkeswell road, cross the River Otter, and take the first turn right. Woodhayes is the first drive on the left.

WOODHAYES
Owners: Christy and Noel Page Turner
Honiton
Devon EX14 0TP
tel: (01404) 42011
3 rooms with private bathrooms
From £30 per person
Open March to mid-December
Children over 15
Wolsey Lodge

Sitting at the heart of the peaceful village of Hornton, the 17th-century Manor House is the exquisite home of Vicki and Malcolm Patrick and their three children. The elegant drawing room is set aside for guests use and meals are taken in the beautifully appointed, beamed dining room. Winter, decked out in soft tones of peach, is a delightful bedroom. Sweet peas decorate the bedlinen in the Crows Nest, an aptly named, snug attic room with exposed stone walls and a huge beam running across its floor. Across the courtyard part of the stables has been converted into an adorable, two-bedroom, one-bath cottage which can be rented as self-catering or on a bed-and-breakfast basis. Vicki is happy to prepare dinner or directs guests to one of the numerous village pubs that serves excellent food. Guests are welcome to use the impressive gymnasium or swim in the swimming pool. The Manor House is ideally situated for visiting Stratford-upon-Avon, Warwick Castle, and the Cotswold villages. Upton House, with its amazing collections of old masters paintings, Brussels tapestries, porcelain figures, and 18th-century furniture, is popular, as is the glorious Elizabethan home Charlcote and its surrounding park. *Directions:* From Banbury take the B4100 signposted Gaydon for ½ mile, then turn left for Horley and Hornton. In Horley turn right to Hornton. In 2 miles turn left for Hornton. Drive down the hill and The Manor House is on the left, opposite the village school.

THE MANOR HOUSE
Owners: Vicki and Malcolm Patrick
The Green
Hornton, Banbury
Oxon OX15 6BZ
tel: (01295) 670386
4 rooms, 2 with private bathrooms
From £25 per person
Open all year
Children welcome

Behind the tile-hung facade of Rixons lies a home that dates back to Tudor times, full of beams and low ceilings, with an inglenook fireplace and a snug, paneled study. Jean and Geoffrey dine with their visitors at the long refectory table, joining them afterwards for coffee and conversation round the fire. The galleried guestroom is open to the rafters with its bedroom downstairs and a sitting room and the bathroom on the balcony above. Honey-colored beams, country pine furniture, and sprigged bedcovers make the twin-bedded room, tucked under the eaves, a delight. Horsted Keynes has a lovely old church built as a replica of one in Cahagnes, France by a Norman nobleman after the Battle of Hastings. By appointment you can visit The Forge, an adjacent museum containing artifacts of North American Plains Indians. On weekends and in the summer vintage steam trains run between Horsted Keynes and Sheffield Park which is especially beautiful in spring when the rhododendrons and azaleas are in bloom. *Directions:* From East Grinstead (adjacent to Gatwick) take the A22 south through Forest Row and beyond for 2 miles to the Roebuck Hotel where you turn right for Danehill. At Danehill turn right and follow signs for Horsted Keynes. Rixons is opposite the post office.

RIXONS
Owners: Jean and Geoffrey Pink
Lewes Road
Horsted Keynes
West Sussex RH17 7DP
tel: (01825) 790453 fax: (01825) 790122
2 bedrooms with private bathrooms
From £27 per person
Closed Christmas and New Year
Children over 12
No Smoking house
Wolsey Lodge

In 1248 John D'Jeu came from France to establish a farm here and over the years the locals corrupted the name to Jews Farm. You enter the house through a decorative, warm peach hallway that leads into the lofty dining room with its walk-in fireplace, long, polished oak table, sturdy chairs, and small paned windows that overlook an idyllic green valley. The adjacent drawing room enjoys the same view though the focus of the room is the enormous fireplace where a blazing log fire crackles. Sarah and John are the most welcoming of hosts and if guests do not wish to eat in they direct them to nearby country pubs and restaurants that they enjoy. Upstairs the bedrooms are decorated to the highest of standards. The pink room with its lovely brass and iron double bed has an ensuite bathroom while the other bathroom is made private for either of the other large twin-bedded rooms. This unspoilt region of narrow lanes bordering green fields contrasting with open moorlands, with picture-postcard villages nestling in sheltered valleys is relatively free of holiday traffic. *Directions:* Leave the M5 at exit 25 (Taunton) and follow signs for Barnstaple (B3227) to Wiveliscombe where you turn right at the traffic lights then right at the White Hart pub signposted Huish Champflower. After 2 miles, at the top of a steep hill, turn right down a narrow lane and Jews Farm House is the second turning on the left.

JEWS FARM HOUSE
Owners: Sarah and John Fox
Huish Champflower
Wiveliscombe, Taunton
Somerset TA4 2HL
tel: (01984) 24218
3 rooms, 2 with private bathroom
From £28 per person
Closed December and January
Children over 10
Wolsey Lodge

Set in a valley carved by a stream rushing down from high, bleak moorlands, Hutton le Hole is a cluster of pale stone houses, a picturesque village in the heart of the spectacular North Yorkshire Moors National Park. The lintel above the Hammer and Hand's doorway declares the date of the house, built as a beer house for the iron workers, as 1784. Now it is home to Alison, formerly a lawyer, and John, once a London policeman, and their son Giles who happily welcome guests to their bed and breakfast. John's passion for cricket explains the old cricket prints hanging in the dining room and the bar. Tucked behind the dining room (dinner is available except on Tuesdays and Thursdays) is a minute bar offering just enough room for a drink before dinner. The gentle tick of a huge grandfather clock and the crackle of a blazing log fire welcome you to the sitting room. A steep, narrow staircase leads to three snug bedrooms, each prettily decorated to give a feeling of light and warmth. Alison finds that Cook's Cabin, a pocket-sized attic room with heavy ships' beams supporting the steeply sloping ceiling, is very popular despite the inconvenience of negotiating a narrow, twisting staircase to use its bathroom on the floor below. Hutton le Hole houses the Ryedale Folk Museum which is well worth a visit. York is less than an hour's drive away. *Directions:* Take the A170 from Thirsk towards Pickering. The left-hand turn to Hutton le Hole is signposted just after Kirbymoorside. The Hammer and Hand is at the heart of the village.

HAMMER AND HAND GUEST HOUSE
Owners: Alison and John Wilkins
Hutton le Hole
York
Yorkshire YO6 6UA
tel: (01751) 417300
3 rooms with private bathrooms
From £20 per person
Closed Christmas
Children welcome

The magnificent scenery of the Lake District, the Yorkshire Dales, and Hadrian's Wall are within easy driving distance of Hipping Hall, so visitors can easily justify a stay of several days in Jocelyn Ruffle and Ian Bryant's comfortable home. Guests help themselves to pre-dinner drinks from the honesty bar in the conservatory which links the main part of the house to the Great Hall where dinner is served. A soaring, beamed ceiling and a broad oak plank floor provide an impressive setting for the excellent five-course meal served around one large table where guests are looked after by Ian while Jos creates in the kitchen. Ian selects wine to complement each course. The bedrooms are named after local hills and dales, and all are comfortably and very tastefully furnished, often with lovely old pieces bought at local auctions. Each has its own sparkling new, well equipped bathroom. The four acres of garden are a delight and feature a large expanse of lawn set up for croquet and a kitchen garden which provides many of the vegetables enjoyed at dinner. Two suites, named Emily and Charlotte after the Bronte sisters who attended school in Cowan Bridge, occupy a courtyard cottage. They each have a kitchen and living room downstairs, bedroom and bathroom upstairs. *Directions:* Leave the M6 at junction 36 and follow the A65 through Kirkby Lonsdale towards Skipton. Hipping Hall is on the left, 3 miles after Kirkby Lonsdale.

HIPPING HALL
Owners: Jocelyn Ruffle and Ian Bryant
Cowan Bridge
Kirkby Lonsdale
Cumbria LA6 2JJ
tel: (015242) 71187 fax: (015242) 72452
5 rooms with private bathrooms (+2 suites)
Double from £75
Open March to November
Credit cards: EC, MC, VS
Children over 12

As long ago as 1290 Penisale market was held here but by the 1980s, all that was left of the community of Penisale was the shell of a farm and an ancient barn at the end of a rutted track. A local entrepreneur demolished the barn and incorporated its aged beams and stones into his vision of an Elizabethan farmhouse which he intended to be the center of a leisure complex. The venture went bankrupt and was purchased by Ann and Philip Unitt. They have done the most magnificent job of removing the "Las Vegas" aspects of the conversion and making this one of the premier bed-and-breakfast establishments in South Yorkshire. Splurge and request the Alderman's suite and you're treated to a queen-sized bed, set in an alcove beneath massive beams, and a decadent bathroom complete with enormous tub. The three other bedrooms are small only by comparison. Dine in on the night of your arrival, as the manor is rather off the beaten track. Breakfast is usually served in the pine kitchen. The Peak District is on your doorstep and the countryside is very reminiscent of Bronte country which is about an hour's drive away. *Directions:* Leave the M1 at junction 35a and take the A616 (10 miles) to Langsett. Turn right opposite the Wagon and Horses pub and, at the cross roads, turn sharp right, then go right at the Y. When you see Brockholes Lane on the left, turn right and follow the farm track for 2/3 mile.

ALDERMANS HEAD MANOR   **NEW**
Owners: Ann and Philip Unitt
Hartcliffe Hill Road
Langsett, Stocksbridge
South Yorkshire S30 5GY
tel and fax: (01226) 766209
4 rooms with private bathrooms
From £22.50 per person
Closed Christmas
Children over 12
No Smoking House

Treffry Farmhouse was for many years the major farm on the vast Lanhydrock estate. Now Lanhydrock is the principal National Trust property in Cornwall and Treffry Farmhouse is home to Pat and David Smith. This is very much a working farm where the cows come up the lane every morning and guests are welcome to watch the milking. There are often children around (usually in the woodland adventure playground) for the old barns in the farmyard are now lovely, self-catering cottages that range from small and tidy (Granary Steps) to large and luxurious (Linhay). The farmhouse offers bed-and-breakfast accommodation in three flowery little bedrooms (Green, Pink, and Cream), each named for the color of their decor. Guests have a pine-paneled sitting room and country-style breakfast room. A three-minute walk brings you to Lanhydrock where you get a real sense of "upstairs downstairs" as you tour the richly furnished Victorian main rooms, maids' bedrooms, and fabulous kitchen with its enormous copper pans and old-fashioned dairy cooled by a little stream. Treffry Farmhouse is perfect for exploring Cornwall's northern (St Ives, Tintagel and, Boscastle) and the southern coasts (St Michael's Mount, Polperro, and Mousehole). *Directions:* From Bodmin, take the B3268 towards Lostwithiel to the mini-roundabout where you turn right. The farm is on your right after 300 yards.

TREFFRY FARMHOUSE   **NEW**
Owners: Pat and David Smith
Lanhydrock
Bodmin
Cornwall PL30 5AF
tel and fax: (01208) 74405
3 rooms with private bathrooms
From £19 per person
Open all year
Children over 6
No Smoking house

The Farmhouse Hotel and Restaurant is very much a Rouse family operation: Dad (Don) runs the dairy farm, Mum (Mary) operates the farmhouse as a hotel, son Wesley is the hotel manager, and daughter-in-law Nikki is the chef. Surrounded by its outbuildings and facing a large garden, this 17th-century Cotswold stone farmhouse has been tastefully converted while retaining the cozy charm of its walk-in fireplaces, oak beams, and low ceilings. Bedrooms are named after Oxford colleges and range from small attic rooms with dormer windows (Trinity and Keebles) to a luxurious double where the soft pink color of the walls and carpet is picked up in the flower-sprigged drapes and ornate bedhead. Nuffield is a ground-floor room equipped for the handicapped. The restaurant has been extended from the beamed farmhouse dining room into a Victorian style conservatory. Dinner begins with hors d'oeuvres followed by soup and sorbet. The main course is a choice of roasts or two specials. The Farmhouse is a very informal place: I know of no other hotel where guests can ask to visit the cows being milked. Oxford and Woodstock are just a short drive away. *Directions:* University Farm is on the A4095 (Faringdon road) 3 miles south of Witney. Unfortunately, RAF Brize Norton is nearby, so be prepared for some aircraft noise.

THE FARMHOUSE HOTEL AND RESTAURANT
Owners: The Rouse Family
University Farm, Lew
Bampton
Oxon OX18 2AU
tel: (01993) 850297
6 rooms with private bathrooms
From £25 per person
Closed Christmas
Credit cards: EC, MC, VS
Children over 5

Tucked in an unspoiled valley high above the hustle and bustle of the more well-known Lake District tourist routes, this traditional pub lies surrounded by the ruggedly beautiful Lakeland scenery. Built of somber-looking slate in 1872 as a resting place for travelers, the hostelry is still a base for tourists, many of whom come here for the walking. They gather by the bar, the sound of their hiking boots echoing hollowly against the slate floor, poring over maps and discussing the day's activities. By contrast, the carpeted and curtained dining room and lounge with its velour chairs seem very sedate. The Stephenson family pride themselves on the quality of their food and offer a five-course meal in addition to substantial bar meals. Do not expect grand things of the accommodations as this is not a luxury establishment. But, for travelers who enjoy quietly decorated, simply furnished, and spotlessly clean rooms with modern bathrooms, the Three Shires fills the bill. Just a few miles away are some of the Lake District's most popular villages: Hawkshead, Ambleside, Coniston, and Grasmere. *Directions:* From Ambleside take the A593, Coniston road, cross Skelwith Bridge, and take the first right, signposted The Langdales and Wrynose Pass. Take the first left to Little Langdale and the Three Shires Inn is on your right.

THREE SHIRES INN
Owners: The Stephenson Family
Little Langdale
Ambleside
Cumbria LA22 9N2
tel: (015394) 37215
11 rooms, 7 with private bathrooms
From £28 per person
Closed January
Children welcome

Built in 1673 as a rectory, Landewednack House sits above the 6th-century church and a cluster of thatched cottages which lead down to the rocky inlet of Church Cove at the tip of the Lizard peninsula. Newly restored to a state of luxury unknown to former residents, Landewednack House was purchased in 1994 by Marion and Peter Stanley who fell in love with the house, its walled garden and magnificent views. Guests are welcomed with a traditional Cornish tea of scones, clotted cream, and strawberry jam served in the elegant sitting room. In the evening guests dine together in the dining room before a log fire in the massive 17th-century fireplace. Upstairs, the large yellow bedroom's windows frame the church and the sea. The other two bedrooms are furnished with antiques and one has its Jacuzzi bathroom across the hall. This southern-most spot in England is far from the crowds. Walk along the clifftops to the adorable village of Cadgwith where fishermen pull their boats high up the shingle beach and from where you can accompany the lobster fishermen. *Directions:* From Helston, take the A3083 to Lizard and turn left before entering the village, signposted Church Cove and Houselbay. Take the next left turn, signposted Church Cove and Lifeboat Station, and Landewednack House is on your left through the large granite gateposts.

LANDEWEDNACK HOUSE **NEW**
Owners: Marion and Peter Stanley
Church Cove
Lizard
Helston
Cornwall TR12 7PQ
tel: (01326) 290909 fax: (01326) 290192
4 rooms, 3 with private bathrooms
From £25 per person
Closed Christmas
Children over 12
No Smoking house

The village of Llanmynech straddles the border between Wales and England, making it the perfect location for exploring both Shropshire and North Wales. In order to make their home more spacious, Carol and Bryan Fahey have combined two small front rooms into a guest dining and sitting room with a log fire for colder weather. The house was for many years the village Dame School and a photo of the class of 1904 hangs in the hallway. Up the narrow staircase are three attractive bedrooms (the single and twin are snug and cottagey while the double is large enough to accommodate a lovely Victorian half-tester bed). The guestrooms share a bathroom and a shower room. If visitors are staying for several days, Carol can sometimes assign private facilities. As a retired catering lecturer Carol offers a high standard of cuisine at moderate cost, which she feels contributes to her having so many return guests. Bryan, a keen fly-fisherman, is happy to give advice and make fishing arrangements for guests. The Faheys are keen walkers, as are many of their guests who come to hike along Offa's Dyke and enjoy walking beside the Montgomery Canal. A lovely day out in Wales could include visiting Llanrhaeder waterfall and a drive around Lake Vyrnwy. *Directions:* From Oswestry, take the A483 towards Welshpool for 5½ miles to the village of Llanmynech. Turn left on the B4398 toward Knockin and after ¼ mile cross the humpback bridge and Vyrnwy House is the fourth house on the left.

VYRNWY BANK   **NEW**
Owners: Carol and Bryan Fahey
Llanmynech
Shropshire SY22 6LG
tel: (01691) 830427
3 rooms sharing 2 bathrooms
From £14 per person
Open February to December
Children welcome

Neil and Judy Burns Thomson came to the wide, flat vistas of Norfolk so that Neil could start a landscaping and garden maintenance company: his first project was to plant the verges of their long driveway with saplings. They have an easy, friendly way about them that makes guests feel right at home and life is very informal here. Neil and Judy are happy for guests to join them for supper, they join them for pre-dinner drinks in the sitting room, dine with them in the flagstone dining room at the large trestle table, and enjoy conversations afterwards over coffee. Dating from Tudor times, the house has lots of charming features such as exposed beams and low, sometimes sloping ceilings. Neil and Judy have cleverly removed the plasterwork between two rooms to make a spacious sitting room with the old wooden supports intact as a decorative partition between seating areas. The two double bedrooms at the top of the steep, narrow staircase are cottage-cozy, yet spacious, and have exposed beams and white plasterwork. Pretty floral fabrics adorn the bedspreads and matching curtains. The two bedrooms share a spacious bathroom and Judy is happy to make certain guests have private facilities by just renting one room. It is a short drive into Norwich to view its splendid 12th-century keep, now the Castle Museum, and to visit Norwich Cathedral. *Directions:* Long Stratton is 10 miles south of Norwich on the A140. Turn left past the church into Hall Lane and Mayfield Farm is on the right after a mile.

MAYFIELD FARM
Owners: Judy and Neil Burns Thomson
Long Stratton
Norwich
Norfolk NR15 2RX
tel: (01508) 31763
2 rooms sharing 1 bathroom
From £20 per person
Closed Christmas
Children over 12

When the Richards bought this house they were unaware that their cottage-style home with its maze of little rooms was in fact a medieval great hall with giant wooden beams and roof trusses. Careful restoration has revealed the large parlor below and the great hall above. While the parlor with its mullioned windows, beamed ceiling, and sofas arranged before the huge stone fireplace causes guests to "ooh and aah," it is the great hall that makes them gasp as they regard the massive roof trusses and the maze of intricate timberwork soaring overhead. The soft glow of flickering candlelight bathes guests as they dine at the refectory table in the great hall. Cozy, beamed bedrooms are decorated to perfection in country print fabrics and have accompanying bathrooms neatly tucked under the rafters. The garden, which is completely encircled by a wide moat, has a willow-shaded fish pond which is home to lazily swimming ducks. Nearby Shrewsbury with its twisting lanes, castle, and open-pillared market hall deserves exploration. Farther afield are the Ironbridge Gorge Museum and the historic town of Ludlow. *Directions:* From Shrewsbury take the A49 south for 8 miles: Longnor is signposted to the left. Go through the village past the school and turn left into the lane marked "No Through Road." When the lane turns left Moat House is straight ahead.

MOAT HOUSE
Owners: Margaret and Peter Richards
Longnor
Shrewsbury
Shropshire SY5 7PP
tel: (01743) 718434
3 rooms with private bathrooms
From £32 per person
Open April to October
Credit cards: All major
Children not accepted
Wolsey Lodge

This endearing cottage dates back to the early 14th century when it was home to a yeoman farmer. With its little upstairs windows peeking out from beneath a heavy thatch roof and its timber-framed wall fronted by a flower-filled garden, Loxley Farm presents an idyllic picture. The picturebook ambiance is continued inside where guests have a tiny parlor and dine together round a long table in the low-beamed dining room. Up the broad polished stairs is a suite of rooms consisting of a child's bedroom, bedroom, and bathroom. With their beams, and sloping ceilings and floors these provide the premium accommodation. Across the garden a timbered building has been converted to provide more contemporary accommodation: a bedroom at either end with a living room and kitchen between. Breakfast is the only meal served and guests often walk into Loxley to dine or go to The Bell in Alderminster. A quiet back road brings you into the center of Stratford-upon-Avon, birthplace of the greatest poet in the English language, William Shakespeare. There are historical timbered buildings to investigate, lovely shops and the Royal Shakespeare Theatre. In nearby Shottery is Anne Hathaway's picturebook cottage. Warwick Castle and Coventry Cathedral are both easily visited from Loxley. *Directions:* Loxley is signpost off the A422 Stratford-upon-Avon to Banbury road about 4 miles from Stratford on the left. Go through the village to the bottom of the hill and turn left (Stratford-upon-Avon) and Loxley Farm is the third house on the right.

LOXLEY FARM
Owners: Anne and Rod Hornton
Loxley
Warwickshire CV35 9JN
tel: (01789) 840265
3 rooms with private bathrooms
From £21 per person
Closed for Christmas
Children welcome

This elegant Georgian townhouse was built in 1770 and designed by Sir James Gibbs of Radcliffe Library (Oxford) and St Martins in the Fields (Trafalgar Square) fame. Michael and Guy have decorated their home with great flair, and added the most enviable collection of paintings and antique furniture. A great deal of effort is put into the evening meals. Breakfast is ordered the night before and served promptly at the time of your choosing. Stairs wind up to the sitting rooms and up again to the bedrooms (there are lots of stairs and no lift). While the principal bedroom sports a decorative, wrought-iron and brass bed, I preferred the adjacent spacious twin-bedded room. Further up the house a suite of rooms is ideal for three people traveling together (no reduction for children). If you're up to the climb, there's a sweet little bedroom under the eaves. Guests are not given door, or room keys. Ludlow, its castle, marketplace, and shops are on your doorstep. Stokesay Castle and Powys Castle and garden are great attractions as are the nearby towns of Worcester and Shrewsbury. *Directions:* Take the one-way system through Ludlow almost to the castle gates. With the walls on your right, turn left down Dinham and look for the three burgundy-colored doors. There is unrestricted parking on the street.

NUMBER ELEVEN   **NEW**
Owners: Guy Crawley and Michael Martin
Dinham
Ludlow
Shropshire S78 1EJ
tel: (01584) 878584
4 rooms with private bathrooms
From £28 per person
Open all year
Children over 12
No Smoking house

The Salweys of Shropshire can trace their lineage hereabouts back to 1216 and The Lodge has been in their family since it was built in the early 1700s, but it is definitely not a formal place. Guests are likely to find Hermione in her wellies in the garden or dressed in jeans preparing dinner for her guests and family. She puts guests at ease, encouraging them to feel as though they are friends of the family, and enjoys pointing out the architectural details of the house and explaining who's who amongst the family portraits. In the evening, guests gather in the morning room and help themselves to drinks from the honesty bar before going into dinner at a spectacular long table made of burled wood, made especially for the house. Up the grand staircase the three large bedrooms are most attractive: Chinese has a suite of furniture painted in an Asian motif, Roses is a large double with an enormous bathroom, and The Yellow Room is a large twin with its bathroom across the hall. The nearest tourist attraction is the medieval town of Ludlow with its old inns, alleyways of antique shops, Norman castle, and riverside walks. *Directions:* Leave Ludlow over Ludford Bridge traveling south. After 1½ miles turn right on the B4361 signposted Richards Castle. After 400 yards turn right through the entrance gates of The Lodge by a curved stone wall, and continue up the long drive to the house.

THE LODGE
Owners: Hermione and Humphrey Salwey
Ludlow
Shropshire SY8 4DU
tel: (01584) 872103
3 rooms with private bathrooms
From £32 per person
Open April to October
Children not accepted
Wolsey Lodge

How unusual to find an outstanding Elizabethan Manor amidst the suburbs and how lucky that this manor is a 15 minute drive from Heathrow Airport making it absolutely perfect for your first and last nights in England if you are visiting from overseas. Carved faces by the massive front door, bowed leaded windows, paneling and beams make this the most impressive of homes where the warmest of welcomes is offered by Bar and her sister Sue. Relax in the oak-paneled sitting room or curl up in the upstairs hallway nook with a cup of tea and biscuits. Bedrooms are delightful: the large paneled double has an ensuite shower, the twin is decorated in sunny lemons and has its bathroom across the hall, and the small double room has a little sitting area in the tall bay window which overlooks the lovely garden. For dinner guests often walk to the pub down the road. Maidenhead railway station is only a mile away and a 30 minute train ride finds you in London—ideal for the theater or sightseeing. Windsor, Henley on Thames and Marlow are 15-minutes drive while Oxford is 45-minutes. *Directions:* Leave the M4 at junction 8/9 and take the A404 (M) to junction 9A signposted Cox Green. Follow the Cox Green signs at both mini-roundabouts into Cox Green Road. Turn left at the Foresters pub and Beehive Manor is on your right in 600 yards.

BEEHIVE MANOR **NEW**
Owners: Bar Barbour and Sue Lemin
Cox Green Lane
Maidenhead
Berkshire SL6 3ET
tel: (01628) 20980
3 rooms with private bathrooms
From £27.50 per person
Closed Christmas
Children over 12
No Smoking house

For centuries Barracott farm has been tucked in a gentle hillside overlooking Hayne Down and Hound Tor at the heart of Dartmoor. This wild and beautiful area is now a national park and Barracott the home of Val and Jim Lee. Guests enter this stone house via the Alpine garden and through a Dutch door into the broad hallway and cozy guests' sitting room where guests are served a spectacular, mouth-watering, multi-course breakfast including homemade yogurt and fresh-baked bread. From the sitting room, a doorway opens to a little staircase which leads up to the two cottage-style bedrooms, simply decorated with matching drapes and bedspreads (one ensuite and one down the hall). For dinner you are directed to The Kestor in Manaton or the Rock Inn in Haytor Vale. Falling under the spell of this lovely spot, visitors often walk Easdon Moor, which rises behind Barracott, to explore its hut circles which are the ancient foundations of Bronze Age homes. The wild beauty of Dartmoor with its sheltered villages and market towns has a magic all its own; with deep valleys, rushing streams, and wild moorlands. Buckfast and Buckland Abbeys, National Trust properties such as Castle Drago, the Devonshire coast, and Cornwall are among the sightseeing possibilities. *Directions:* From Exeter take the A38 to the A382, Bovey Tracy, turnoff. At the second roundabout turn left following signs for Manaton. Go through Manaton, and, beyond the village, turn left at the T junction and then take the first right to Barracott.

BARRACOTT
Owners: Val and Jim Lee
Manaton
Newton Abbot
Devon TQ13 9XA
tel: (01647) 22312
2 rooms with private bathrooms
From £22.50 per person
Open April to October
Children welcome if family takes both rooms

Conjecture has it that Thomas Hardy used Old Lamb House (then the Lamb Inn) as Rollivers Tavern in *Tess of the d'Urbervilles*. Jenny and Ben continue the tradition of hospitality by offering accommodation to guests in two large front bedrooms that share a bathroom. Guests use the front door (while family use the kitchen door) and atop the curving staircase there's a sitting area with two armchairs and lots of tourist information. Jenny finds that most guests prefer to relax in their bedrooms, both of which contain comfortable, old-fashioned armchairs. The Pink Room is decked out in soft pinks with matching flowery bed-linen and drapes, while the Gray Room is outfitted in soft blue-grays and offers lovely views of the garden with its stately cedar tree. Guests usually drive the short distance to the Crown or the Blackmore Vale pubs for dinner. Restaurant-goers are directed to Jesters in Shaftesbury. Dorset abounds in country lanes that lead to pretty villages such as Milton Abbas and Cerne Abbas with its club-wielding giant carved into the chalk hillside. Shaftesbury has many steep roads running down into Blackmore Vale, the most famous being Gold Hill, a steep, cobbled street. *Directions:* From Shaftesbury, take the A30 towards Exeter for 4 miles to East Stour. Turn left on B3092 to Marnhull (3 miles) and go half a mile beyond Marnhull church where you turn right at the triangle of grass with a signpost and into Old Lamb House's driveway.

OLD LAMB HOUSE   **NEW**
Owners: Jenny and Ben Chilcott
Marnhull
Dorset DT10 1QG
tel: (01258) 820491 fax: c/o (01258) 473939
2 rooms sharing 1 bathroom
From £17 per person
Closed Christmas
Children welcome
No Smoking house

Mungrisdale is one of the few unspoilt villages left in the Lake District and is made up of a pub, an old church, and a cluster of houses and farms set at the foot of rugged, gray-blue crags. Do not confuse The Mill with the adjoining pub, The Mill Inn: park next to the pub and walk through the adjacent garden to arrive at this cozy hotel. Rooms are of cottage proportions: a small lounge with comfy chairs gathered round a blazing log fire, a cozy dining room where each small oak table is set with blue napkins, candles, willow pattern china, and a tiny flower arrangement, and nine small bedrooms with matching draperies and bedspreads. Most visitors are attracted here for the outstanding dinners prepared by Eleanor. Dinner consists of an appetizer followed by a tasty homemade soup served with soda bread (the latter a popular fixture on the menu), a main course (with a vegetarian alternative), dessert, and cheese and biscuits. Bed and breakfast only bookings are not usually accepted. The Lake District is a beautiful region, popular with walkers and sightseers alike. Some of its premier villages are Coniston, Hawkshead, Sawrey (home of Beatrix Potter), Ambleside, and Grasmere. *Directions:* Leave the M6 at junction 40 and take the A66 towards Keswick for 10 miles. The Mill is 2 miles north of this road and the signpost for Mungrisdale is midway between Penrith and Keswick.

THE MILL HOTEL
Owners: Eleanor and Richard Quinlan
Mungrisdale
Penrith
Cumbria CA11 0XR
tel: (017687) 79659
9 rooms, 7 with private bathrooms
From £41 per person dinner, bed and breakfast
Open February to October
Children welcome

In her younger years Beatrix Potter used to visit Ees Wyke House with her family. Now it is a very pleasant hotel run by Mag and John Williams who have painted and decorated the house from top to bottom in a comfortable style. They are constantly improving the standards at their hotel, the latest project being the addition of a large dining room with glorious views across the countryside. John, a former cookery teacher at a catering college, enjoys cooking. His dinner menu always offers choices of starter, main courses, and desserts. The bedrooms have tall windows framing gorgeous countryside views and many overlook nearby Esthwaite Water. Tucked under the eaves, two airy, spacious attic bedrooms have super views: one has a bathroom ensuite while the other has a private bath just next door. The other bedrooms also have a mix of ensuite and adjacent bathroom arrangements. The smallest bedroom, on the ground floor, is reserved for visitors who have difficulty with stairs but unfortunately has no view. A short stroll up the village brings you to Hill Top Farm where Beatrix Potter wrote several of her books. Walks abound in the area and the more oft-trod Lakeland routes are easily accessible by taking the nearby ferry across Lake Windermere. *Directions:* From Ambleside take the A593 towards Coniston. After about a mile turn left on the B5286 to Hawkshead. Skirt Hawkshead village and follow signs for the ferry. Ees Wyke House is on the right just before Sawrey.

EES WYKE COUNTRY HOUSE HOTEL
Owners: Mag and John Williams
Near Sawrey
Hawkshead, Ambleside
Cumbria LA22 0JZ
tel: (015394) 36393
8 rooms with private bathrooms
From £36 per person
Closed January
Children over 10 and babies

The quiet, narrow country lane that runs in front of Fosse Farmhouse is the historical Fosse Way, the road built by the Romans to connect their most important forts from Devon to Lincolnshire. Caron Cooper has furnished her rooms with great flair using soft colors and enviable country French antiques in every room. Charming collectibles and country china adorn much of the sitting and breakfast rooms and most pieces are for sale. Upstairs there are three extremely comfortable guest bedrooms. My favorite was The Pine Room with its mellow pine furniture and especially spacious, luxuriously equipped bathroom. Across the courtyard, the ground floor of the stables has been converted to a tearoom and restaurant. On the floor above, three cottage-style bedrooms are stylishly decorated in white on white. With advance notice, Caron enjoys preparing an imaginative, three-course dinner, and is happy to cater to vegetarian palates. At Christmas time Caron offers a three-day festive holiday. This tranquil countryside setting is within an easy half-hour's drive of Bath, Bristol, Tetbury, and Cirencester and the picture-perfect village of Castle Combe is also nearby. *Directions:* Exit the M4 at junction 17 towards Chippenham, turn right on the A420 (Bristol road) for 3 miles to the B4039 which you take around Castle Combe to The Gib where you turn left opposite The Salutation Inn. Fosse Farmhouse is on your right after 1 mile.

FOSSE FARMHOUSE
Owner: Caron Cooper
Nettleton Shrub, Nettleton
Chippenham
Wiltshire SN14 7NJ
tel: (01249) 782286 fax: (0249) 783066
6 rooms with private bathrooms
From £40 per person
Open all year
Credit cards: All major
Children welcome

Set in the picturesque moorland village of North Bovey, frequent winner of the best kept Dartmoor village award, Gate House has a lovely location just behind the tree-lined village green. The location and warm welcome offered by hosts Sheila and John Williams add up to the perfect recipe for a countryside holiday. The sitting room has an ancient bread oven tucked inside a massive granite fireplace beneath a low beamed ceiling, and the adjacent dining room has a pine table in front of an atmospheric old stove. A narrow stairway leads up from the dining room to two of the guest bedrooms, each with a neat bathroom tucked under the eaves. The third bedroom is found at the top of another little staircase, this one off the sitting room, and affords views through a huge copper beech to the swimming pool (unheated) that guests are welcome to use, and idyllic green countryside. Sheila prepares a lovely country breakfast and four-course evening meal (including vegetarian dishes if requested). Apart from walking on the moor and touring the moorland villages, many guests enjoy golf at the nearby Manor Hotel. The Devon coastline is easily accessible and many guests enjoy a day trip into Cornwall, often venturing as far afield as Clovelly. *Directions:* From Exeter take the A38 to the A382, Bovey Tracy turnoff. Turn left in Mortenhampstead onto the Princetown road, then immediately left again to North Bovey, down the lane into the village and Gate House is on the left beyond the Ring of Bells.

GATE HOUSE
Owners: Sheila and John Williams
North Bovey
Devon TQ13 8RB
tel: (01647) 40479
3 rooms with private bathrooms
From £22 per person
Closed Christmas and February
Children over 15

Rectory Farm was purchased by Robert's grandparents in 1915. While Robert continues the family farming tradition, his wife Mary Anne offers bed-and-breakfast accommodation in their lovely Elizabethan farmhouse. Mary Anne and Robert have put a lot of effort into tastefully modernizing and refurbishing their very old home. Guests have a small sitting and breakfast room with a woodburning stove. Upstairs, a modern shower room has been added to the large twin-bedded room where you sleep beneath an unusual ceiling whose support beam is covered in decorative plasterwork—a lovely fireplace was unearthed during the remodeling. A smaller pine double bedroom has an ensuite shower room and sits among the family's bedrooms. Breakfast is the only meal served, so guests often enjoy dinner at the Red Lion pub in the village or the Harcourt Arms in nearby Stanton Harcourt. The farmlands border the River Thames and you can walk along the Thames path and go fishing. An hour's drive will find you in Stratford-upon-Avon or Bath. Closer at hand, you can tour the Oxford colleges, try your hand at punting, and visit Blenheim Palace where Churchill was born. *Directions:* From Oxford, take the A420 (Swindon) to Kingston Bagpuize, turn right on the A415 (Witney), cross the river and turn immediately right beside the Rose Revived car park. After 2 miles turn right at the T junction, and Rectory Farm is on the right beside the church.

RECTORY FARM   **NEW**
Owners: Mary Anne and Robert Florey
Northmoor
Witney
Oxfordshire OX8 1SX
tel: (01865) 300207
2 rooms with private bathrooms
From £18.50 per person
Open February to mid-December
Children over 14
No Smoking house

The Grange, a former rectory, is a rambling Regency home covered with wisteria, comfortably furnished by Sue and Malcolm Whittley. Guests are welcome to use the formal drawing room overlooking the vast expanses of sweeping lawn and mature trees or the cozy television room. The four bedrooms range in size from a large twin room softly carpeted in pink with light pink walls and cushioned windowseats, to a compact double room with sunny yellow walls prettily furnished in country pine. Homey touches such as hanging bouquets of dried flowers, pictures on the walls, and even a Paddington bear on a corner shelf add warmth. Amidst the five acres of lawns and gardens, tucked behind the kitchen garden and beyond the ducks and peacocks, is a walled swimming pool. Northwold is within easy reach of Norwich with its splendid castle museum and cathedral, the ancient university town of Cambridge, the medieval market town of King's Lynn, and the unspoilt, scenic North Norfolk coast. Nearby are the Royal Family's summer home, Sandringham House, the Caley Mill lavender farm, and the church in Heacham where John Rolfe married his Indian princess, Pocohontas. *Directions:* From King's Lynn take the A134, signposted Thetford, to Northwold. Turn left into the village, pass the church and the Old Rectory (on the left) and turn left in front of the row of cottages which brings you into The Grange's driveway.

THE GRANGE
Owners: Sue and Malcolm Whittley
Northwold
Thetford
Norfolk IP26 5NF
tel: (01366) 728240
4 rooms, 2 with private bathrooms
From £17 per person
Closed Christmas
Children over 5

While The Plaine is the name of this guesthouse, it also is the name of the area of the village that was used for centuries as the market place. Sadly, the days of markets are long gone and the market cross has been dismantled so that large trucks can negotiate the village streets. Fortunately, evenings are quiet and you can enjoy the village's lovely old buildings. Guests have a snug sitting room and dine together round the long dining-room table where breakfast is the only meal served. For dinner The George and the Fleur de Lys serve good food in atmospheric pubs dating back to medieval times. One bedroom is on the ground floor, while the other two are found up a circular stone staircase. The bedrooms are all about the same size and have reproduction four-poster beds draped in flowery fabrics that coordinate with the curtains. Norton St Philip is an ideal location for visiting Georgian Bath with its wealth of attractions and Wells with its magnificent cathedral set in spacious grounds. During the quiet evening hours you can follow a walking tour that leads you round the village. *Directions:* From Bath, take the A367 (Exeter road) and at the end of the dual carriageway turn left on the B3110 signposted Frome. Go through the villages of Midford and Hinton Charthouse to Norton St Philip where you find The Plaine on your left opposite the George pub.

THE PLAINE GUEST HOUSE   **NEW**
Owners: Gill and Terry Gazzard
Norton St Philip
Bath
Avon BA3 6LE
tel: (01373) 834723 fax: (01373) 834101
3 rooms with private bathrooms
From £23.50 per person
Open all year
Credit cards: all major
Children welcome
No Smoking house

The river estuaries around Plymouth provide sheltered harbors for sailboats. Bobbing yachts fill the inlets, narrow lanes wind around wooded headlands, and the shores are lined with pretty, pastel-washed homes. Rowan Cottage has been Jeannie's home for many years and she has turned what was a pocket-sized home into a spacious habitation. The large double-bedded room's ceiling rises to the rafters and has a door in the bathroom that leads into the flower-filled garden. A snug single room, all decked out in blue and white, has its bathroom across the hall. Jeannie and Guy are very casual, very warm hosts who join their guests for dinner and conversation, settling them afterwards with coffee and chocolates in the large beamed sitting room with its views across the estuary. If guests prefer, they will direct them to local pubs and restaurants that serve excellent food. Guy and Jeannie can arrange to take you sailing on their 32-foot Moody. Famous voyagers, such as the Pilgrim Fathers and Captain Cook, who set out on historic journeys are commemorated in nearby Plymouth. *Directions:* Leave the A38 (Exeter to Plymouth road) at the sign to Yealmpton and Ugborough. Continue to Yealmpton and take a left fork to Noss Mayo (3½ miles). Keep the river on your right all the way to Bridgend Quay, and Rowan Cottage is the first cottage on your left, up the lane.

ROWAN COTTAGE
Owners: Jeannie and Guy Hollebone
Bridgend, Noss Mayo
Plymouth
Devon PL8 1DX
tel: (01752) 872714
2 rooms with private bathrooms
From £29 per person
Closed for Christmas
Children over 12
No Smoking house
Wolsey Lodge

Jane and Robin Halfhead take only one party of guests at a time in their lovely home because Jane feels that it is important that guests not share a bathroom with people they do not know. The two very pretty guestrooms consist of a twin-bedded room and an airy room where the twin beds can be zipped together to make a king-sized bed. In the morning, guests enjoy breakfast in front of the Aga at a country-pine table beneath the kitchen beam decorated with dried hops. In the evening, Jane and Robin join their guests for a drink before dinner and dine with them round the dining-room table. The tariff for dinner includes wine and a pre-dinner drink. Beyond the lovely house the garden opens up to miles of very gently-rolling countryside. Guests are welcome to use the tennis court or enjoy a game of croquet on the lawn. Oaksey is on the southernmost edge of the Cotswolds and guests often visit the old market towns of Tetbury and Malmesbury with their lovely buildings and attractive shops. Farther afield lie Bath and Cheltenham. *Directions:* From Cirencester, take the A429 towards Malmesbury for 6½ miles, passing through Kemble, and turn left at the crossroads for the 2-mile drive to Oaksey. Go through the village and Oaksey Court is the second-to-last house on the right.

OAKSEY COURT **NEW**
Owners: Jane and Robin Halfhead
Oaksey
Malmesbury
Wiltshire SN16 9TF
tel: (01666) 577265
2 rooms sharing 1 bathroom
From £25 per person
Closed Christmas and New Year
Children over 10
No Smoking house
Wolsey Lodge

Lise and Michael Hilton have done the most magnificent job of converting a 17th-century barn and stable into an exquisite home. Huge timbers reach to the apex of the hayloft in the living room where high-backed sofas are drawn cozily round the fire, a baby grand piano occupies an alcove and the room opens up to a vast billiard room that Lise and Michael encourage guests to enjoy. Lovely pictures and plate collections adorn the walls, and enviable antiques furnish every nook and cranny. Two bedrooms are found up the main staircase in the guest wing: the romantic pine room has a four-poster bed and ensuite shower room while the lovely twin-bedded room has its bathroom just next door. Across the courtyard the carriage house is a luxurious suite with a sitting room and bedroom. Lise and Michael are the most gracious of hosts, and enjoy helping guests plan their sightseeing and dining. Unspoiled Suffolk villages are close at hand, Constable country is within easy reach as is Dunwich, the medieval village that has almost been claimed by the sea, the elegant seaside resort of Southwold, Minsmere Bird Reserve, and the concert hall at Snape. Sample local wines at the Bruisyard St Peter winery in the village of Bruisyard—you may come away with a case. *Directions:* Otley is 6 miles northeast of Ipswich. With the Post Office on your right Bowerfield is on your right after a quarter mile. Lise will send or fax you detailed driving instructions.

BOWERFIELD HOUSE   **NEW**
Owners: Lise and Michael Hilton
Otley
Ipswich
Suffolk IP6 9NR
tel: (01473) 890742 fax: (01473) 890059
4 rooms with private bathrooms
From £22 per person
Open March to November
Children over 12

Jean and Jack Langton are the most delightful, attentive hosts, and Jean is an accomplished cook who always offers her guests a splendid dinner, or if they prefer a less substantial meal, supper. Jean and Jack dine with their guests around the prettily set dining-room table that overlooks their large back garden. Set in a charming countryside village, The Old Rectory began life as two tiny cottages, home to the vicar's coachman and the butler. At the turn of the century the cottages were combined and became the vicarage. Parkham's vicar liked to change residences—there are three old rectories in the village. The Langtons' home is decorated in a light, airy way and while it does not abound in antiques, there is a traditional feel to the house. The largest double bedroom overlooks the garden as does a smaller double room, which has its private bathroom across the hall. Guests seek out Jean in the kitchen and chat around the Aga planning their sightseeing excursions which invariably include the Royal Horticultural Society gardens, Rosemoor in Torrington, and Marwood Hill with its national collection of astibes. Clovelly, the famous, somewhat over-commercialized village, is a great attraction, as is the Dartington glass factory in Torrington. *Directions:* From Bideford take the A39 south to Horns Cross (Coach and Horses inn) and turn left for Parkham. Turn left by the church and left at the second turning on the right. At The Bell pub turn left and The Old Rectory is on your right halfway down the hill.

THE OLD RECTORY **NEW**
Owners: Jean and Jack Langton
Parkham Nr Bideford
Devon EX39 5PL
tel: (01237) 451443
3 rooms with private bathrooms
From £35 per person
Closed Christmas
Children over 12
No Smoking house

Penryn is a very much a working town whose main thoroughfare, Broad Street, runs up the hill from the fishing quay. Half-way up the hill, fronting directly onto the street, you find Clare House. Built in the 17th century as an impressive gentleman's residence, it was restored several years ago by Jean and Jack Hewitt who ran the town's newsagents for many years. Jean is chatty and friendly and, while guests have their own spacious sitting room, she often whisks them to her side of the house where she and Jack join them for tea and a chat in their sitting room or in the Victorian conservatory with its hundred-year-old grapevine. Jean finds that having bed-and-breakfast guests has expanded her circle of friends from the town to the world. Bedrooms at the front of the house are particularly large: one has its shower cubicle and sink in the room and the loo across the hall while the other has its private bathroom across the hall. The third bedroom is quietly located at the back of the house and has ensuite facilities. A small refreshment room (stocked with tea, coffee, soft drinks, and biscuits), is located between the bedrooms. Guests often walk to the Waterfront restaurant or drive to the Pandora, an adorable, thatched inn overlooking Restronguet Creek. *Directions:* From Truro, take the A39 toward Falmouth. Follow the second signpost to Penryn and turn right at the traffic lights on the quay into Broad Street, Clare house is on the left.

CLARE HOUSE   **NEW**
Owners: Jean and Jack Hewitt
20 Broad Street
Penryn
Cornwall TR10 8JH
tel: (01326) 373294
3 rooms with private bathrooms
From £22 per person
Closed Christmas and New Year
Children over 12
No Smoking house

While Prospect House's location is commercial (it's next to a telephone exchange, and opposite a car showroom), the house is set back from the main road and enjoys a large garden. The lane that runs beside it meanders past fishermen's cottages to the main street of Penryn which climbs the hill from the harbor to the unusual long, narrow town hall that sits in the middle of the road. Cliff and Barry forsook their careers in teaching and theater management to run this attractive guesthouse. The comfortable sitting room has an intricate plasterwork frieze bordering the ceiling while the dining room, which was at one time the kitchen, retains its large fireplace and uneven flagstone floor. Barry and Cliff commissioned a handsome dining-room table to match the delicate Flemish dining chairs. The three bedrooms are named after clipper ships that sailed from Penryn harbor. Waterwitch, the most spacious bedroom, overlooks the pretty garden and has a large bathroom. On the landing there is a refreshment area where you can make tea and coffee or select juices, soft drinks, and ice from the refrigerator. Cornwall has an abundance of secluded river estuaries (Helford estuary was Daphne du Maurier's Frenchmans Creek), an abundance of gardens (Trelissick, Glendurgan, Trebah), and friendly villages down switchback lanes. *Directions:* From Truro take the A39 towards Falmouth, then the B3292. Ignore the first signpost into Penryn—Prospect House is on the corner opposite the Volvo dealership.

PROSPECT HOUSE
Owners: Barry Sheppard and Cliff Paul
1 Church Road
Penryn
Cornwall TR10 8DA
tel and fax: (01326) 373198
3 rooms with private bathrooms
From £23.50 per person
Open all year
Children over 12

Swale Cottage is down a tiny country lane on the outskirts of Penshurst. Here Cynthia Dakin spent a year converting an 18th-century barn into a pretty home. Everything is cottage-cozy with white-painted walls and black beams. Cynthia's paintings (many of them of local scenery) decorate the walls. Breakfast is the only meal served on the oak refectory table and guests often go to the George and Dragon in Speldhurst (reputedly one of England's oldest pubs) or the Castle Inn in the pretty village of Chiddingstone. Upstairs, the bedrooms are cottagey in their decor and, while the four-poster is the largest room, I preferred the smaller double with its brass and iron bedstead and small bathroom. A twin bedroom has its bathroom across the hall. Guests enjoy a walk across the fields to Penshurst Place with its magnificent Tudor garden. It's a ten-minute drive to Hever Castle (Anne Boleyn's childhood home) and Chartwell (Churchill's home). The information packet in the rooms contains a useful chart which outlines the prices, times and days of opening of the most popular 20 houses, castles, and gardens in the area. *Directions:* From Tunbridge Wells, take the A26 north for 2½ miles and turn left onto the B2176 to Penshurst (3 miles). Turn left into Poundsbridge Lane, and, after 100 yards, right into a narrow lane signposted Swale Cottage.

SWALE COTTAGE   **NEW**
Owner: Cynthia Dakin
Old Swaylands Lane
off Poundsbridge Lane
Penshurst
Kent TN11 8AH
tel: (01892) 870738
3 rooms with private bathrooms
From £25 per person
Open all year
Children over 10
No Smoking house

There was a farm on this site recorded in the Domesday book of 1086, though the present farm and its outbuildings date from the 1500s. Anthony's family have farmed here for generations and, while he concentrates on all things farming, Lynne concentrates on the upscale bed-and-breakfast that she runs in a wing of the farmhouse and the converted stables. When I visited her, she was poring over ideas for her fifth bedroom to be built in a tiny cottage in the stableyard. This (like the other rooms in the house) will not be your typical farmhousey-style accommodation. Lynne plans to decorate her new cottage in darker Mediterranean colors and furnish it with hand-painted furniture. The rooms I saw were furnished with pastel-painted furniture that coordinates with the draperies and bedspreads, giving a light, airy feel. Bathrooms and shower rooms are sparklingly modern and one sports a clawfoot tub and separate shower. Lynne loves to eat out and enjoys discussing dining plans with guests. She also has a folder on restaurants and traditional pubs in the area. The idyllically pretty seaside villages of Fowey, Looe, and Polperro are great attractions as are the National Trust houses of Cotehele and Lanhydrock. *Directions:* From Looe take the A387 signposted Polperro. Before you arrive in Polperro Trenderway Farm is signposted to your right.

TRENDERWAY FARM   **NEW**
Owners: Lynne and Anthony Tuckett
Pelynt
Polperro
Cornwall PL13 2LY
tel: (01503) 72214
4 rooms with private bathrooms
From £26 per person
Closed Christmas and New Year
Children not accepted
No Smoking house

A humorous, tongue-in-cheek "rule" book is found in every bedroom at Bales Mead and woe betide you if you do not comply. The illustrations are drawn by Peter Clover, who with his partner Stephen Blue, runs a very tight ship in their exceptionally attractive home. Guests enjoy a sophisticated sitting room complete with log-burning fireplace and baby grand piano. Upstairs the bedrooms are named after villages in the Porlock vale. Selworthy is cool in lemon and blue with outstanding ocean views. Bossington is all in pink, white, and mulberry with a view of the shingle beach and distant headland. Allerford is smaller and overlooks the garden and woodlands. Each queen-bedded room has a sink tucked neatly in the corner and the three rooms share the facilities of a bathroom and an additional loo. Breakfast is the only meal served (promptly at 9:00 am). Stephen and Peter recommend excellent local pubs and restaurants for dinner. In the '50s the house was owned by a well-known horticulturist who filled the garden with specimen plants from all over the world. Just across the lane are vast stretches of shingle beach. Bales Mead is in the hamlet of West Porlock between the pretty village of Porlock and the picturesque harbor of Porlock Weir. Rising behind the house are the vast expanses of Exmoor. *Directions:* From Minehead, take the A39 to Porlock, then a right turn to Porlock Weir takes you a short distance to West Porlock, where you find Bales Mead on the left.

BALES MEAD   **NEW**
Owners: Stephen Blue and Peter Clover
West Porlock
Somerset TA24 8NX
tel: (01643) 862565
3 rooms sharing 1½ bathrooms
From £22 per person
Closed December and January
Children not accepted
No Smoking house

The lifeboatman has been known to deliver guests, and their luggage, to Fort Cottage when there's an especially high tide. While this is an adventure for visitors, Carol takes the sea coming up the road as a natural part of living beside the harbor in Old Portsmouth. When she suspects the sea may be paying a visit she simply removes the rugs from the tile floor in the little downstairs bedroom and mops the floor when the tide ebbs. This attractive room is decorated in pink candy stripes and has a small ensuite shower room. Curl up on the window seat in the airy upstairs sitting room and watch the Isle of Wight ferries and the fishing boats come and go. On the top floor two small pretty bedrooms have tiny ensuite shower rooms (request the front room with its harbor view). For dinner, Carol makes suggestions on the pubs and restaurants that are within walking distance. Take the waterbus (Easter to November) across the harbor to tour Nelson's flagship, *HMS Victory*, Henry VIII's ship, *Mary Rose*, and *HMS Warrior,* an 1861 iron-clad battleship, then go on to the submarine museum. *Directions:* Exit the M27 at junction 12, signposted Portsmouth and ferries. Follow signs for IOW car ferry through the center of the town, then look for a brown signpost (at a roundabout) to Cathedral and Old Portsmouth. Pass the cathedral and at the end of the road turn right. Fortitude Cottage is on your left.

FORTITUDE COTTAGE   **NEW**
Owner: Carol Harbeck
51 Broad Street
Old Portsmouth
Hampshire PO1 2JD
tel: (01705) 823748
3 rooms with private bathrooms
From £20 per person
Closed Christmas
Credit cards: EC, MC, VS
Children over 16

FWe SAT'S

A narrow country road runs through Nidderdale (one of Yorkshire's quietest and most attractive dales) to Ramsgill, a village of a few stone houses. The Yorke Arms is tucked next to the village green with the dale rising through stone-walled fields to the high moorlands. The hotel is full of old-world charm with its polished stone flag hallway, snug little bar, traditional residents' lounge, and large restaurant with high-backed Windsor chairs and enormous dresser decorated with pewter and china. Bedrooms are spacious and each is accompanied by a sparkling bathroom or shower room. The two superior rooms are huge in size and sport comfortable seating areas and extra-large bathrooms. A good value for money is the package that includes dinner, bed, and breakfast (two or more nights). You can take beautiful walks from the hotel which vary in length from strolls by the nearby reservoir to day-long hikes over the moorlands. The ruin of Fountains Abbey, founded by Cistertian monks in 1132 and dissolved by Henry VIII, is an awesome sight and walking paths abound. A magnificent drive takes you from Grassington through Littondale to Malham Cove (one of Yorkshire's most celebrated natural features) and back to Grassington. Nearby Harrogate is an 18th-century spa town. *Directions:* From Ripon, take the B6285 to Pateley Bridge where you turn right at the signpost for Ramsgill. Ramsgill is the first village after the reservoir.

THE YORKE ARMS   **NEW**
Managers: Kay and Colin MacDougall
Ramsgill by Harrogate
North Yorkshire HG3 5RL
tel and fax: (01423) 755243
13 rooms with private bathrooms
From £34.50 per person
Open all year
Credit cards: EC, MC, VS
Children welcome

The Burgoyne family were people of substance hereabouts for they secured the premier building site in this picturesque Swaledale village and built an impressive home that dwarfs the surrounding buildings. Gone are the days when one family could justify such a large home and now it's a welcoming hotel run by Derek Hickson and Peter Carwardine. Derek makes guests feel thoroughly at home while Peter makes certain that they live up to their motto "Tis substantial happiness to eat." Peter prepares a fixed-price, four-course meal every evening with plenty of choices for each course. The handsome lounge is warmed by a log fire in winter and full of inviting books on the area. There's abundant scope for walking and driving in this rugged area using Reeth as your base, though you'll be hard pressed to find a lovelier Dales view than that from your bedroom window of stone-walled fields rising to vast moorlands (one bedroom faces the back of the house). Redmire and Marrick are the premier rooms, being larger and more spacious. Robes and slippers are provided for the occupants of Keld and Thwaite who have to slip across the hall to their bathrooms. Richmond with its medieval castle and the Bowes Museum, near Barnard Castle, with its fine collection of French furniture and porcelain are added attractions. *Directions:* From Richmond take the A6108 towards Leyburn for 5 miles to the B6270 for the 5-mile drive to Reeth. The Burgoyne Hotel is on the village green.

THE BURGOYNE HOTEL
Owners: Derek Hickson and Peter Carwardine
Reeth
North Yorkshire DL11 6SN
tel and fax: (01748) 884292
8 rooms with private bathrooms
From £65 double
Closed January
Credit cards: EC, MC, VS
Children welcome

Until 1990, Shawswell was a working farm in a sheltered valley beyond the little village of Rendcomb. Now it is a countryside retreat where the only sounds you hear are birdsong and the bleating of sheep which graze in the fields beyond the garden. David and Muriel Gomm have done a lovely job of keeping all the cottagey aspects of the farmhouse—the old kitchen stove in what is now the dining room, the farmhouse latch doors, and the beamed ceilings and walls. Sofas and chairs are drawn round the fire in the sitting room and it is here that David serves drinks in the evening. Upstairs, uneven corridors lead to the bedrooms where you can choose from a snug single, a twin with a huge bathroom, or a spacious, four-poster Jacobean room. Dinner is available with advance notice. A 3-mile walk will find you at the Roman villa of Chedworth or the villages of Withington or Colesbourne. Within an hour's car journey are the interesting towns of Bath, Cheltenham, Gloucester, Stratford-upon-Avon, and Oxford. *Directions:* From Cirencester, take the A435 towards Cheltenham for 5 miles and turn right into the village of Rendcomb. Keep on this road (which becomes a single-track lane as it leaves the village) for 1½ miles and you come to Shawswell Country House (do not turn off the tarmac).

SHAWSWELL COUNTRY HOUSE   **NEW**
Owners: Muriel and David Gomm
Rendcomb
Cirencester
Gloucestershire GL7 7HD
tel: (01285) 831779
5 rooms with private bathrooms
From £22.50 per person
Open February to November
Children over 10

Whashton Springs Farm is a perfect base for exploring the Yorkshire Dales. A five-minute drive finds you at the foot of Swaledale in Richmond, with its cobbled market square and Norman Castle perched high above the river. The farm is run by Gordon Turnbull and his two sons who grow corn and potatoes and run a herd of hill cows and sheep. Spring is an especially good time to visit, for the little lambs are kept close to the farm. Fairlie welcomes guests to the farmhouse and offers accommodation within the large sturdy house or in one of the delightfully private bedrooms that open directly onto the courtyard. A wing of the barn has been converted into a most attractive self-catering cottage for families who want to stay for a week. A Yorkshire farmhouse breakfast and very reasonably priced dinners are served in the dining room. Gordon serves the dinners, which gives you an opportunity to ask questions about the farm. On Sunday evenings guests are directed to local pubs and restaurants in Richmond for dinner. Within an hour you can be in Durham, York, or the Lake District. The Yorkshire Dales are on your doorstep and the North Yorkshire Moors just a half hour distant. *Directions:* From the A1, take the A6136 to Richmond. Turn right at the traffic lights signposted for Ravensworth and follow this road for 3 miles to the farm, which is on your left at the bottom of a steep hill.

WHASHTON SPRINGS FARM   **NEW**
Owners: Fairlie and Gordon Turnbull
Richmond
North Yorkshire DL11 7JS
tel: (01748) 822884
8 rooms with private bathrooms
From £21 per person
Open February to mid-December
Children over 5

Shearings is an adorable 16th-century thatched cottage sitting beside a winter stream in one of the prettiest villages in Hampshire, right on the edge of the New Forest. Positively bursting with old-world charm, the interior of Shearings has blackened oak beams, large inglenook fireplaces, and sloping floors. In fact, one of the most charming prospects of a stay here is the fact that there is not a straight wall or even floor in the house. For the duration of their stay Colin, a retired army brigadier, and his wife Rosemary adopt guests as family, joining them for pre-dinner drinks, dinner, coffee, and conversation in front of the fire. A cocktail, wine, and coffee are included in the cost of the three-course dinner. Rosemary aims to provide good English cooking and guests can expect traditional choices such as roast lamb and lemon meringue pie. The bedrooms are pretty: one has a bathroom ensuite and a single and double room share a bathroom. Across the garden The Outback has its bedroom under the eaves and a bathroom and kitchenette on the ground floor. Salisbury is a short drive away and Stonehenge and the New Forest are within easy reach. *Directions:* From Salisbury take the A354 towards Dorchester and after Combe Bissett (5 miles) turn left for Rockbourne. Shearings is on the left in the village, reached by a little bridge that spans the stream.

SHEARINGS
Owners: Rosemary and Colin Watts
Rockbourne
Fordingbridge
Hampshire SP6 3NA
tel and fax: (01725) 518256
3 rooms, 1 with private bathroom
From £24 per person
Open February to November
Children over 12

Few English guesthouses offer the ambiance, warmth, and welcome of Mizzards Farm, a lovely, 16th-century farmhouse built of stone and brick. The setting is peaceful: the River Rother flowing through the thirteen acres of gardens and fields and the driveway winding through the large meadow-like front lawn past a small pond. The heart of the house, where breakfast is served, is especially inviting, with one wall filled by a massive inglenook fireplace and a staircase leading up to an open minstrels' gallery. In a newer wing, a sophisticated lounge is nicely furnished with antiques and highlighted by a grand piano. Twice a year concerts are held here. The home was previously owned by an English rock star who converted the largest bedroom into a glitzy, but fun theatrical showplace with electric curtains operated from the bed on a grand dais and a marble bathroom featuring a double bathtub. The other two guestrooms are smaller and are pleasantly decorated in more traditional decor. Dinner is not served but there are many excellent choices of places to eat nearby. For the athletically minded, Mizzards also has a covered swimming pool for guests' use. *Directions:* From Petersfield take the A272 towards Midhurst. Turn right at the crossroads in Rogate, follow the road for ½ mile, cross the narrow bridge over the river and take the first right on the small lane up to Mizzards Farm.

MIZZARDS FARM
Owners: Harriet and Julian Francis
Rogate
Petersfield
Hampshire GU31 5HS
tel: (01730) 821656 fax: (0730) 821655
3 rooms with private bathrooms
From £22.50 per person
Closed Christmas
Children over 6
No Smoking house

With a backdrop of mountain peaks and a lush green lawn sweeping down towards Rosthwaite village, The Hazel Bank hotel has a superb location in Borrowdale, one of the loveliest and quietest Lake District valleys. The owners, Gwen and John Nuttall, have renovated this large Victorian residence, adding modern conveniences such as sparkling bathrooms to the bedrooms to create a small comfortable hotel, all the while keeping the house's period charm and character. All the rooms are light, airy, and uncluttered. The bedrooms are named after nearby mountains. The largest rooms are Scafell Pike, a twin-bedded room that overlooks the beginning of the Scafell range, and Great Gable where a four-poster bed and two substantial armchairs overlook the mountains through large windows. A traditional English dinner is served at 7:00 pm and a houseparty atmosphere prevails. John does most of the cooking and a measure of his success is the great number of returning guests, so bookings for one night or bed and breakfast only are not usually accepted. This is walking country so the hotel has a drying room for clothing and is happy to provide packed lunches. *Directions:* The hotel is located 7 miles south of Keswick on the B5289. Turn left over the little humped-back bridge just before entering Rosthwaite village.

HAZEL BANK
Owners: Gwen and John Nuttall
Rosthwaite
Borrowdale
Keswick
Cumbria CA12 5XB
tel: (017687) 77248
6 rooms with private bathrooms
From £43 per person dinner, B and B
Open mid-March to November
Children over 6
No Smoking house

This solid stone cottage in the tiny village of Rowland is home to Mary Everard and her sleek black labrador Meg. Mary returned to her home area after living in the United States for several years and converted her holiday home into an adorable little bed and breakfast. The large hall, paneled in golden oak with its matching staircase leading to the bedrooms, was once the living room of a much smaller cottage. Warmed in winter by a wood burning stove, the hall opens up to a country-style dining room with a long, polished table and a softly carpeted sitting room with an array of brass fire equipment on the hearth. At the top of the stairs two prettily decorated twin bedrooms with views across the garden share a bath/shower room (with a separate loo). Mary asks guests to select their breakfast the night before so she can have it hot and ready, right on time. Bread is always homemade and yogurt and stewed fruit are available as well as the more usual cooked fare. The nearby Peak District National Park is a walker's paradise and the countryside offers picturesque walled fields and sturdy stone villages, highlighted in the summer when the villagers decorate their wells with floral designs. Also in the vicinity are Bakewell with its antique and tea shops and Monday market, Chatsworth House, and medieval Haddon Hall. *Directions:* Leave Bakewell over the bridge and follow the Hathersage road to Hassop. At Hassop, turn left up the hill for Rowland. After half a mile turn right and Holly Cottage is on the right.

HOLLY COTTAGE
Owner: Mary Everard
Rowland
Bakewell
Derbyshire DE45 1NR
tel: (01629) 640624
2 rooms sharing 1 bathroom
From £18 per person
Closed November and December
Children welcome

Rye is a delightful town and we offer Green Hedges as a place to stay if you do not want to be in the quaint, cobbled town center. Set on a very quiet street with private parking (the no entry signs discourage non-residents), Green Hedges is a large Edwardian home that has been renovated and refurbished so that guests have one half of the house and Sheila and John Luck and their family have the other. Guests have a small sitting room with games and books (there are televisions in the rooms) and a breakfast room overlooking the large garden which terraces down to a swimming pool and vast expanse of lawn. Breakfast (the only meal served) offers lots of choices including omelets, pancakes with maple syrup and spicy cheese on wholemeal toast. Upstairs the three bedrooms are simply decorated and each has a small ensuite shower room. If you prefer a bath, there's a bathroom across the hall. It is a fifteen-minute walk into town and if you choose to drive, Sheila will direct you along a back-road (go early, parking is scarce). *Directions:* Arrive in Rye on the A268 (London road). Go down Rye Hill and turn right where the circular white sign with red letters states "private road, no entry, no through road." Green Hedges is on your left. (If you cross the railway line you have gone too far.)

GREEN HEDGES   **NEW**
Owners: Sheila and John Luck
Hillyfields
Rye Hill
Rye
East Sussex
tel: (01797) 222185
3 rooms with private bathrooms
From £27.50 per person
Closed Christmas
Credit cards: EC, MC, VS
Children over 12
No Smoking house

Our cover picture Rye, a busy port in medieval times, has become marooned 2 miles inland since the sea receded. Once the haunt of smugglers who climbed the narrow cobbled streets laden with booty from France, Rye is now a picturesque town which invites tourists to walk its cobbled lanes. On Rye's most historic street, Jeake's House dates back to 1690 when it was built by Samuel Jeake as a wool storehouse (wool was smuggled to France while brandy, lace, and salt were brought into England). From the street you enter a small reception which leads to a rather formal looking parlor and bar which opens up to a large galleried hall, now the dining room, where a roaring log fire blazes in winter. At some point in its history the house was owned by the Baptist Church who built this room as a chapel. From the spacious attic bedroom, to the romantic four-poster room, and the snug single, no two rooms are alike. All are most attractively decorated and furnished with antiques in keeping with the historical mood of the house. All offer modern amenities such as teamaking trays, television, and telephone and all but two have ensuite bathrooms. Within easy driving distance are Winchelsea, Battle Abbey (built on the site of the Battle of Hastings in 1066), Bodiam Castle, and Sissinghurst gardens. *Directions:* Rye is between Folkestone and Hastings on the A259. Mermaid Street is the main street in town and Jeake's House is near the Mermaid Inn.

JEAKE'S HOUSE
Owners: Jenny and Francis Hadfield
Mermaid Street
Rye
Sussex TN31 7ET
tel: (01797) 222828 fax: (01797) 222623
12 rooms, 10 with private bathrooms
From £26.50 per person
Open all year
Credit cards: all major
Children welcome

Rye is one of England's most enchanting towns and Little Orchard House is one of Rye's most engaging small bed and breakfasts. The location is ideal, right in the heart of town on a small lane leading off Mermaid Street. Don't miss the inn's discreet sign. An archway frames a most inviting little courtyard faced by a pretty cottage with a tan-colored door. Inside there is no formal reception area: registration takes place in the cozy, country style kitchen which opens onto a very large old-fashioned walled garden. In one corner rises a red brick tower, once used by smugglers to signal if the coast was clear. Here there is a spacious ground-floor room and atop the tower a snug, four-poster room with panoramic views. The tower can be rented on a self-catering basis. Bedrooms in the house are equally attractive: Lloyd George is masculine and gracious, the four-poster Garden Room romantic, and the Hayloft cottagey with pine and wicker. The very friendly owners, Sara and Robert, are very involved in the management of their bed and breakfast and personally see that each guest is made welcome and pampered. To learn more about Rye's fascinating history attend the sound and light show at the Rye Town Model, then set out to explore with a walking tour of the town. *Directions:* Follow signs to the town center and enter via the old Landgate Arch. West Street is the third street on the left off the High Street (ignore the "authorized traffic only" signs).

LITTLE ORCHARD HOUSE
Owners: Sara Brinkhurst and Robert Bird
West Street
Rye
Sussex TN31 7ES
tel: (01797) 223831
5 rooms with private bathrooms
From £30 per person
Open all year
Credit cards: EC, MC, VS
Children over 12

Atop the quaint cobbled streets of Rye is the ancient church and churchyard of St Mary's, surrounded by a square of delightful old houses. Fortunately for visitors to this picturesque town, one of these, The Old Vicarage (a dusty pink Georgian house with white trim and twin chimneys), is run as a guesthouse by a delightful young couple, Julia and Paul Masters. You can be certain of a proper cuppa here as Julia is a tea-blender and has devised a special blend of tea for her guests. Since Julia and Paul bought The Old Vicarage they have been constantly upgrading and refurbishing the rooms. All of the guestrooms are decorated with Laura Ashley fabrics: two have contemporary four-poster beds and one has a coronet-style draped headboard. Each of the guestrooms has color television, hairdryer, and tea tray. There are also some small, rooms tucked under the eaves on the top floor. The garden suite, a large family room with a sitting area, is below stairs. The ambiance throughout the bed and breakfast is one of homey comfort. Overnight car parking is provided across the square in a residents-only parking area. If you write ahead, the Masters will send you a brochure with a map on just how to find them amongst the maze of Rye's narrow cobblestoned streets. Rye deserves a visit of several days to explore its narrow, cobbled streets, antique and craft shops, and old fortifications. *Directions:* Rye is on the A259 between Folkestone and Hastings.

THE OLD VICARAGE GUEST HOUSE
Owners: Julia and Paul Masters
66 Church Square
Rye
Sussex TN31 7HF
tel: (01797) 222119
6 rooms with private bathrooms
From £19.50 per person
Closed Christmas
Children over 10

Stratford Lodge is tucked down a quiet lane overlooking a large park just a few minutes' drive from the center of Salisbury. Here Jill Bayly has extended her large Victorian home to create a spacious guesthouse but her role as caring hostess and the homey touches make Stratford Lodge feel more a large home than a traditional guesthouse. Pretty wallpapers and fabrics, pastel color schemes, antiques, flowers, and family mementos combine to give the bedrooms a home-like charm and all have a tea tray and biscuits, television, and ensuite bathroom. The downstairs twin and the two large upstairs bedrooms that face the park are particular favorites. Three smaller, more modern, double rooms occupy a wing to the rear of the house. Guests are welcome to walk across the garden to swim in the indoor pool. Jill is an excellent cook and offers a dinner menu with choices: she always has at least one fish dish and one vegetarian main course. Breakfast is a treat and, instead of bacon and eggs, guests may try mushrooms on toast or smoked haddock kedgeree. In addition to Salisbury's old streets and cathedral, Stonehenge and Avebury's megalithic monuments are close at hand while Bath, the New Forest, Winchester, and Southampton are easy day trips. *Directions:* As you enter Salisbury on the A345, from Amesbury, take the second right-hand turn, which is immediately after the Circle K foodstore, onto Park Lane.

STRATFORD LODGE
Owner: Jill Bayly
4 Park Lane, off Castle Road
Salisbury
Wiltshire SP1 3NP
tel: (01722) 325177 fax: (01722) 412699
10 rooms with private bathrooms
From £25 per person
Closed Christmas
Children over 5
No Smoking house

The formal exterior of The Lodge belies the warm decor and friendly welcome which await you indoors. Sally and Roger Dixon's engaging personalities have been imprinted on their home during the three years they spent refurbishing it. Guests can enjoy croquet on the lawn, relax in the Victorian conservatory, or browse through interesting volumes in the comfortable sitting room. Sally is an excellent cook and enjoys serving elaborate dinners in the attractive dining room—the wine list offers a selection of 20 wines. The large principal bedroom has a roomy ensuite bathroom. An equally large blue and yellow twin-bedded room shares a spacious bathroom with a snug single bedroom. Sally is very aware that guests always enjoy their own bathroom facilities, so she rents only one of these bedrooms at a time. Nearby Norwich is rich in historic treasures including a beautiful Norman cathedral topped by a 15th-century spire. The castle, built by one of William the Conqueror's supporters is now the Castle Museum. Between Norwich and the holiday resort of Great Yarmouth lie the Norfolk Broads, full of birdlife and boating enthusiasts. *Directions:* From Norwich, take the A140 signposted for Ipswich for 6 miles, through the village of Newton Flotman which merges into Saxlingham Thorpe. With Duffields Mill on your right, turn left into Cargate Lane signposted Saxlingham Nethergate, and The Lodge is the second driveway on your left.

THE LODGE   **NEW**
Owners: Sally and Roger Dixon
Cargate Lane
Saxlingham Thorpe
Norwich
Norfolk NR15 1TU
tel: (01508) 471422
3 rooms, 2 with private bathrooms
From £27 per person
Open all year
Children over 12

This Suffolk farmhouse stands amidst fields and woods in a quiet country location where for over 400 years it was a working farm. Hostess Mary's caring ways are evident in the quiet, warm way she treats her guests. Her welcome is seconded by handsome George, a tail-wagging dog, and Lizzie, a collie who loves to mother youngsters. Families with children are welcome here, though parents must supervise young ones on the narrow spiral staircase. Mary's old paintings, antique furniture, and books galore fit happily into this mellow, beamed house. Pink-toned armchairs and a long sofa border an Oriental carpet in front of the open log fire in the living room. The food served in the book-lined dining room is excellent: a typical meal might be asparagus and salmon mousse, lamb chops with fresh vegetables and new potatoes, and a choice of desserts. The large principal bedroom has a bathroom ensuite while three smaller bedrooms share a bathroom and an additional WC (with a maximum of six guests at a time the facilities are never overtaxed). Nearby are Blythburgh with its 15th-century church, Dunwich, the medieval village almost claimed by the sea, Southwold, Minsmere Bird Reserve, and the concert hall at Snape. *Directions:* From Ipswich take the A12 (signposted Lowestoft). Between Yoxford and Blythburgh take the lane beside The Happy Eater (on the right) and look for High Poplars on the right after 1½ miles.

HIGH POPLARS
Owner: Mary Montague
Hinton
Saxmundham
Suffolk IP17 3RJ
tel: (0150270) 528
4 rooms, 1 with private bathroom
From £22 per person
Open all year
Children welcome
Wolsey Lodge

Fronting the picturesque River Teign estuary, Shaldon is a most attractive village where every Wednesday, from May to September, residents dress in 18th-century costume, stalls are set on the green, Morris dancers entertain, and docents give guided tours of the village where the early-17th-century Virginia Cottage is one of the oldest residences. Jennifer and Michael Britton sincerely welcome guests to their home. Visitors have their own sitting room where a log fire burns cheerily in the winter and plump sofas and chairs invite you to curl up with a book or enjoy an evening of television. Breakfast is the only meal served and guests usually walk or drive to the Shipwrights Arms pub or Hunter Lodge restaurant. The very large double room can accommodate an extra bed and enjoys views over the garden and a large bathroom. One twin-bedded room has an ensuite bathroom while another has its facilities down the hall. If the weather is warm you can enjoy a refreshing swim in the heated pool. There are lots of National Trust properties within a 30-mile radius. Garden lovers enjoy Plant World where Ray Brown (yes, he's a relative) has planted an interesting geographic garden where each country displays plants native to it. *Directions:* From Exeter take the A380 towards Torquay for 3 miles to the B3192 signposted Teignmouth and Shaldon. Cross over the bridge into Shaldon, follow the main road to your right, and turn at once sharp right, signposted Ringmore. Brook Lane is the third lane on the left and Virginia Cottage is on the right.

VIRGINIA COTTAGE
Owners: Jennifer and Michael Britton
Brook Lane
Shaldon
Devon TQ14 0HL
tel: (01626) 872634
3 rooms with private bathrooms
From £18.50 per person
Closed Christmas
Babies and children over 10

Longdon Manor is an absolutely delightful home tucked deep in the countryside, fronted by rambling outbuildings and picturesque barns, and backed by a grassy garden whose centerpiece is a tall, 17th-century dovecote. The sitting room invites guests to stretch out in a chair before the log fire, gently play the concert grand, or browse through piles of sheet music and books. The polished flagstones, high ceilings, and deeply set mullioned windows echo days long past, for this was a residence as early as the 14th century, with additions being made in the 16th and 17th centuries. The dining room walls are hung with family photos, a deep window niche displays fossils and seashells, and the elegant table is laid with country-style crockery. With advance notice Jane is happy to provide dinner. The bedrooms are all different: a cottage style twin nestles under the eaves, and a double room has Jacobean furniture and a flamboyant bathroom. Although Jane does not usually take reservations on weekends, she often accepts guests who would like to attend one of the informal concerts held here once a month. Longdon Manor is perfect for exploring the Cotswold villages and visiting the theater at Stratford-upon-Avon. *Directions:* From Shipston on Stour take the B4035 towards Chipping Campden. Cross the A429 and after half a mile turn right towards Darlingscott. After a mile the lane bends sharp right while the drive to the manor is straight ahead.

LONGDON MANOR
Owners: Jane Brabyn and family
Shipston on Stour
Warwickshire CV36 4PW
tel: (01608) 682235
2 rooms with private bathrooms
From £35 per person
Open all year Monday to Thursday
Children welcome
No Smoking house

A cozy hilltop refuge from winter storms, an outstanding spring, summer or autumn base for exploring Derbyshire by car or on foot, Dannah Farm is a delightful place for all seasons. The solid Georgian farmhouse is turned over entirely to guests with two cozy sitting rooms furnished with taste and delightful cottagey bedrooms. I particularly liked the two suites which have their private entries from the old stableyard. One has a snug sitting room with an open-tread spiral staircase leading to the low-beamed bedroom while the other is a lofty raftered room with a four-poster bed. Another part of the old stables is a convivial bar and country style restaurant where guests enjoy breakfast and dinner and outside guests are welcomed on Saturday evenings. Adults and children love the animals—the squeaking baby pot-belied pigs are a great attraction. The Peak District National Park is on your doorstep full of walks, bike trails, and appealing little villages. The stately homes Haddon Hall and Chatsworth House are well worth a visit. *Directions:* From Belper take the A517 (Ashbourne road) for 2 miles and after the Hanging Gate Inn take the next right (top of hill) to Shottle (1½ miles). Go straight at the crossroads and after 200 yards turn right into Dannah Farm.

DANNAH FARM   **NEW**
Owners: Joan and Martin Slack
Bowmans Lane
Shottle
Belper
Derbyshire DE56 2DR
tel: (01773) 550273 fax: (01773) 550590
9 rooms with private bathrooms
From £27 per person
Closed Christmas
Credit cards: EC, MC, VS
Children welcome

The Lynch Country House was built for an attorney and his bride in 1812 and was owned by their family for over a hundred years. Roy Copeland purchased the house with the intention of running a country house hotel: however, when the renovations were complete he decided that a bed-and-breakfast was more his cup of tea. Consequently guests get country house style accommodation at bed-and-breakfast prices and Roy gets time to practice his saxophone and clarinet. Roy encourages guests to enjoy the lovely gardens with their topiary hedges and lake with its resident family of black swans. Bedrooms vary in size from snug rooms under the eaves (Alderley is an especially attractive attic room) to Goldington, a large high-ceilinged room with a grand Georgian four-poster bed. Roy supplies a list of restaurants and pubs in each room along with sample menus but finds that guests usually stroll into the village to The Globe pub or Market House Restaurant. Long ago Somerton was the capital of Wessex; today it is a substantial village with some interesting shops and pretty streets lined with old stone houses. Glastonbury, the cradle of Christianity, and Wells with its magnificent cathedral are nearby. Bath is just under an hour away. *Directions:* Exit the M25 at junction 25, taking the A358 towards Chard to the A378 to Langport and straight on to Somerton.

THE LYNCH COUNTRY HOUSE   **NEW**
Owner: Roy Copeland
4 Behind Berry
Somerton
Somerset TA11 7PD
tel: (01458) 272316 fax: (01458) 272590
5 rooms with private bathrooms
From £22.50 per person
Open all year
Credit cards: all major
Children welcome

Speen Cottage is just over an hours' drive from Heathrow airport, most of it via motorway, making this a well-placed starting point for visitors traveling to the west of England. After a refreshing cup of tea guests can relax in the garden, swim in the pool, or take a stroll before dinner. The traditional, bay-windowed sitting room with its soft cream carpet topped with an Oriental rug is light, airy, and spacious and Pamela's stitchery decorates cushions, banners, bellpulls, footstools, and chaircovers. The dining room is furnished with rugged, light-oak furniture from "mouse man" Robert Thompson of Yorkshire, whose small church mouse signature is on each piece. The two twin-bedded rooms have their private bathrooms across the hall, and there is also an additional small single room which, if occupied, shares one of the same baths. In the vicinity are a number of very attractive Berkshire villages and the Vale of the White Horse. A number of historic towns are within an hour's drive: Oxford, Bath, Windsor, Salisbury, Hungerford, and Marlborough. *Directions:* Leave the M4 at exit 13 and take the A34 to Newbury. Then take the A4 west (signposted Hungerford), curve left after the Hare and Hounds then turn immediately left into Speen Lane. In 200 yards enter the large white gates of Speen Cottage on the left.

SPEEN COTTAGE
Owner: Pamela Walsh
Speen Lane
Speen, Newbury
Berkshire RG13 1RJ
tel: (01635) 40859
3 rooms, 2 with private bathrooms
From £22 per person
Open all year
Children not accepted
No Smoking house

This lovely Georgian home set in five acres of grounds in peaceful countryside offers outstanding accommodations. Rashleigh is an enormous room and its double bed has an artfully draped bedhead matching the curtains and bedspread, Treffry is in pink and pine with a frilled corona over the bed, and Prideaux has a dainty, white four-poster bed draped with a pink and white flowery fabric. Each bedroom has an elegant ensuite bathroom with spa bath, tea and coffee makings, television, telephone, and a huge umbrella for guests to use during their stay. Guests have their own entrance into a lofty hallway where double doors open up to a vast sitting room all decked out in warm shades of pale green. Beyond lies a sunny conservatory with wicker chairs and little tables set for breakfast or dinner. Outside are vast rolling lawns, a swimming pool, a hot tub, and a paved terrace with spectacular views across rolling countryside. Local attractions include the picturesque town of Fowey, the fishing village of Mevagissey, the cathedral city of Truro, and Bodmin Moor. Daphne Du Maurier's novel *All the King's Men* is set around St Blazey. *Directions:* Pass over the Tamar Bridge into Cornwall and follow signs to Liskeard. Take the A390 (St Austell turnoff) following it through Lostwithiel and into St Blazey. Cross the railway lines and opposite the Texaco garage turn right into Prideaux Road, following it up the hill to Nanscawen on your right.

NANSCAWEN HOUSE
Owners: Janet and Keith Martin
Prideaux Road
St Blazey, Par
Cornwall PL24 2SR
tel and fax: (0172681) 4488
3 rooms with private bathrooms
From £32 per person
Closed Christmas
Children over 12
No Smoking house

Breathtaking, panoramic views of the Wye Valley open up from Cinderhill House, a pink-washed cottage whose core dates back to the 14th century with additions over the years. Gillie is a warm and friendly hostess who enjoys welcoming guests to her lovely home. Bedrooms in the main house are very prettily decorated and all have tea and coffee trays. An additional attic room with twin beds and a crib is reserved for children so that parents can put their children to bed and go downstairs for dinner. Since my visit Gillie has been busy with the conversion of outbuildings to self-catering accommodation or to be used as extra guestrooms for the house. Two of these rooms have four-poster beds and one self-catering unit has been specially equipped to accommodate wheelchairs. Breakfast is a treat: fruit compotes and cold cereals are followed by hot dishes such as fresh salmon fishcakes and herb omelets, yet Gillie considers dinner her forte! On chilly evenings a crackling log fire invites guests into the large sitting room to enjoy a drink before dinner. Apart from enjoying the peace and quiet of the Wye Valley and the Forest of Dean, guests venture farther afield to Bristol, Cardiff, Gloucester, Cheltenham, Bath, and Hereford. *Directions:* Take the M4 from Bristol over the Severn Bridge to exit 22 for Monmouth. Follow the A466 for 10 miles, turn right over the Bigsweir bridge for St Briavels. Follow the road up and the house is on the left just before the castle.

CINDERHILL HOUSE
Owner: Gillie Peacock
St Briavels
Gloucestershire GL15 6HR
tel: (01594) 530393
5 rooms with private bathrooms
From £22 per person
Open all year
Children welcome

Hilltop has been in host Tim Rathmell's family since it was built in 1640: quite an impressive record! Tim and his wife, Marie Louise, have tastefully modernized the house adding ensuite bathrooms while keeping and exposing lovely features such as the beef loft in the beamed dining room where beef used to be hung to dry above the open fire. They have made the old barn into their home and enjoy welcoming guests to the main house. Four bedrooms with light and airy decor contain spacious king-sized beds and have showers in the bathrooms. The fifth bedroom is a snug, flowery twin and enjoys a large bathroom with a claw-foot tub. Ancient family documents decorate the tiny bar where guests gather to chat over drinks. Tim puts his heart into his cooking and concentrates on properly cooked vegetables and sauces to accompany his main courses while Marie Louise is in charge of dessert which may be a specialty from her German homeland. After dinner guests enjoy the cheer of a blazing log fire in the sitting room or, on warm summer evenings, stretch their legs strolling in the foothills behind Hilltop or down to the village pub. Walks abound in this lovely part of the Yorkshire Dales, and car touring is just as enjoyable, offering castles, country homes, and the abbeys of North Yorkshire. A scenic 70-mile round trip route from Hilltop includes Kilnsey Crag, Malham Tarn, Gordale Scar, and Stump Cross Caverns. *Directions:* Starbotton is in Wharfedale, 16 miles north of Skipton on the B6160.

HILLTOP COUNTRY GUEST HOUSE
Owners: Marie Louise and Tim Rathmell
Starbotton
Skipton
Yorkshire BD23 5HY
tel: (01756) 760321
5 rooms with private bathrooms
From £29 per person
Open mid-March to mid-November
Children welcome

Only the most detailed maps pinpoint Curdon Mill in the hamlet of Vellow, but your endeavors to find this lovely valley close to the sea and near the beautiful Quantock hills are rewarded. The approach to the mill skirts Daphne and Richard Criddle's farm. A few years ago they decided to renovate the old water mill on their property, adding a lounge where guests can relax and browse through books describing sights to see in the area. The mill shaft hangs across the ceiling in the dining room and the restaurant is open to the public. The menu changes daily and there are at least four choices of starter, main and dessert courses. The cheeses are all English and local. Of the six bedrooms my favorites are the Stag Room which was named because deer can sometimes be seen in the fields below the window and the Walnut room named for the walnut bedheads. Regrettably we found the carpets to be somewhat worn. A small swimming pool is secluded on a terrace beside the mill. It's a rural spot where you can enjoy watching the farm animals, taking walks, or even trout fishing. Exmoor National Park is nearby, a region of spectacular scenery that varies from farmland to heathland. *Directions:* Leave the M25 at Taunton junction 25 and take the A358 towards Williton. Do not turn left until you see Stogumber and Vellow signpost together. Curdon Mill is on a sharp right hand bend before you reach Stogumber.

CURDON MILL
Owners: Daphne and Richard Criddle
Lower Vellow, Stogumber
Taunton
Somerset TA4 4LS
tel: (01984) 56522 fax: (01984) 56197
6 rooms with private bathrooms
From £25 per person
Open all year
Children over 10
No Smoking house

The food at The Angel Inn is outstanding and, fortunately for visitors to this pretty part of Suffolk, guests may lodge as well as dine here. When Peter Smith and Richard Wright purchased the inn in 1985 it was in a sorry state, but now its complete refurbishment has transformed it into a building with lots of charm and old-world ambiance. Guests eating in the bar on a weekend are best advised to avoid the crush by arriving early (or just before last orders at 9:00 pm), make their selection from the menu hung on the old, red brick wall above the fireplace, and then settle down at one of the tables grouped under the low-beamed ceiling. Those preferring a more formal meal or quieter atmosphere may elect to dine in the restaurant where tables can be reserved in either of the two dining rooms. One is a cozy room with pine paneling, the other more dramatic, with ceilings removed to expose lofty rafters. Tables are laid with starched linen and soft lighting adds a romantic mood. The menu offers several choices of starters and main courses including a good selection of fresh seafood. Bedrooms are pleasantly furnished and have a light, airy decor. This unspoilt region of quiet countryside offers lots of sightseeing, such as the nearby valley of the River Stour, Dedham, and Flatford Mill, all made famous by John Constable's paintings. *Directions:* Take the A134 Sudbury road from Colchester for 5 miles to Nayland, then turn left for the 2 mile-drive to Stoke by Nayland.

THE ANGEL INN
Owners: Richard Wright and Peter Smith
Stoke by Nayland
Colchester
Essex CO6 4SA
tel: (01206) 263245
6 rooms with private bathrooms
From £28.75 per person
Closed Christmas
Children over 12

There is a moat most of the way round Slough Court, a 14th-century fortified manor house with tiny, mullioned windows set in mellow stone walls beneath a moss-covered roof. Enclosed by the moat is a garden of rolling lawns and overflowing flower beds, a grass tennis court, and a sheltered swimming pool. Across the drawbridge lies the farmyard full of barns and tractors, pigs and cows. Sally is the fourth generation of her family to call Slough Court home, a home that she thoroughly enjoys sharing with her guests. Opposite the great hall with its enormous fireplace is the elegant dining room, the table prettily laid for breakfast with the cereals displayed in giant glass jars. In summer breakfast is the only meal served and guests either walk to the village pub or drive to The Rising Sun, in Knapp, which specializes in fresh fish cuisine. Up the narrow staircase heavy old doors open to attractive bedrooms with tiny, paned windows and exposed wall beams (two are ensuite and one has its bathroom down the hall). If you are interested in farm activities you can watch the cows being milked and discuss the finer points of raising pigs. Basket-making is a traditional Somerset craft and several local farms offer demonstrations and sell baskets. Farther afield lie the towns of Glastonbury and Wells. *Directions:* From Taunton take the A358 towards Chard to the A378 where you turn left towards Langport. In 200 yards turn left onto a country lane signposted North Curry and Stoke St Gregory. Slough Court is on the left in Slough Lane.

SLOUGH COURT
Owner: Sally Gothard
Stoke St Gregory
Taunton
Somerset TA3 6JQ
tel: (01823) 490311 fax: (01823) 490311
3 rooms with private bathrooms
From £22 per person
Open March to November
Children over 12

Bretton House sits beside Fosse Way, the ancient Roman road that runs straight as an arrow through the heart of the Cotswolds. Isolated from the busy thoroughfare by two acres of garden, Bretton House was built at the turn of the century as a rectory. The vicar certainly enjoyed an inspirational view of gently rolling Cotswold countryside from his large rambling home. Barry and Julia bought the house specifically to do dinner, bed and breakfast—putting to good use Barry's training as a cook and his experience managing pubs and restaurants. A pretty pine dining room has little tables and chairs set before tall windows which open up to the garden and the countryside views. For relaxation there is both a smoking and non-smoking sitting room. Up the broad staircase, the bedrooms are named for their decor: Peach has a frilly four-poster, Sweet Pea has airy flowers on the fabric and wallpaper and lovely countryside views, and Fuchsia has blue fuchsia-covered draperies and bedspreads. All have ensuite facilities. Ask to see the enormous, fluffy St Bernards, Megan and Jessie, whose "home" is one of the outbuildings. Bretton House provides an ideal base for exploring the Cotswolds. Within an hour you can be in Stratford-upon-Avon, Warwick, or Oxford. *Directions:* From Stow-on-the-Wold, take the A429 towards Cirencester. Pass a garage on your right and a cemetery on your left, and Bretton House is on your left at the brow of the hill.

BRETTON HOUSE   **NEW**
Owners: Julia and Barry Allen
Stow-on-the-Wold
Gloucestershire GL54 1JU
tel: (01451) 830388
3 rooms with private bathrooms
From £20 per person
Closed Christmas
Children over 10

Alveston Cottage began life over 400 years ago as two one-up-one-down cottages by the River Avon in the heart of Stratford-upon-Avon. Victorian additions melded the tiny dwellings into one and more recently Louise Downing has added her skills to make this unusual house into the most inviting of homes, a home she loves to share with guests. Louise is particularly proud of her art collection where each piece is done by a person she interviewed in the course of her career as a journalist with *The Times*. Louise particularly enjoys preparing old English recipes and offers either dinner or pre- or post-theater supper, serving them in the little parlor with its views through willow branches of the Avon. Upstairs the bedrooms enjoy an uninterrupted view of the river and are particularly attractive with their white on white decor and lacy Victorian pillows. One has an ensuite bathroom while the other has robes provided for trotting to its private bathroom, down the hall. Theater tickets can be arranged and Alveston Cottage is just a few minutes' walk from the Royal Shakespeare Theatre. All the attractions of Stratford (except Anne Hathaway's cottage) are within easy walking distance. Advance reservations are essential. *Directions:* From Oxford take the A34 to Stratford. Before crossing the bridge into town turn right (B4086 to Wellesbourne) opposite the Swans Nest Hotel and Alveston Cottage is the first house on the riverside.

ALVESTON COTTAGE
Owner: Louise Downing
Tiddington Road
Stratford-upon-Avon
Warwickshire CV37 7AE
tel: (01789) 292847
2 bedrooms with private bathrooms
From £29 per person
Open all year
Children over 12

Set behind Tansley village green, Lane End House is, as its name states, the last house in the lane. A house which has been considerably expanded, with a large sitting room whose picture window overlooks the garden. Marion and David Smith used to run a large hotel in Leicestershire and they apply the same professional standards to their guesthouse. Dinner offers choices in all but the main course, and catering to vegetarians is not a problem. David has a large wine list. The emphasis is on low-fat, low sugar foods. At breakfast time, there's homemade muesli, fruit compote, fresh fruit platter and bacon and sausages from the local butcher. A groundfloor bedroom has its bathroom just a few steps away, across the hallway. An open-tread staircase leads up from the dining room to a further three bedrooms, where quite the nicest room has as coronet bedhead draped with pink and green fabric and a bathroom with a clawfoot tub and old-fashioned toilet with its cistern almost at ceiling level. *Directions:* From Matlock, take the A615 Alfreton road for 1½ miles. Enter Tansley village and turn left before the Tavern pub into Church Street. After 500 yards when you see the Gate Inn in front of you, turn right into Green Lane and Lane End House is at the end of the lane.

LANE END HOUSE   **NEW**
Owners: Marion and David Smith
Green Lane
Tansley
Matlock
Derbyshire DE4 5FJ
tel: (01629) 583981
4 rooms with private bathrooms
From £21 per person
Open all year
Credit cards: EC, MC, VS
Children welcome
No Smoking house

TEIGNMOUTH THOMAS LUNY HOUSE Map: 1

Thomas Luny, the marine artist, had this home built in 1792 in the center of Teignmouth just a short walk through narrow streets from the sheltered harbor which has a long history as a fishing and ship-building center. Now this handsome house is home to Alison and John Allan and their two young children. John serves guests pre-dinner drinks before donning the starched, white uniform that both he and Alison wear for serving dinner. In the morning John or Alison brings early morning tea to your room. All the rooms have a television, mineral water, ensuite bathroom, and a lovely old seachest. Each is decorated in a contrasting style: Chinese enjoys a peach and green decor and painted Oriental furniture; Clairmont is pretty in green and yellow; Luny is autumnal in beige and brown; and Bitton contemporary with its impressive four-poster bed. Walk the narrow streets of old Teignmouth to the working harbor and along to the Victorian section of town with its long sandy beach, cheerful pier, and esplanade popular with the bucket-and-spade brigade. Just across the estuary lies Shaldon where every Wednesday, from May to September, residents dress in 18th-century costume. *Directions:* From Exeter take the A380 towards Torquay for 3 miles to the B3192 to Teignmouth. Turn left at the traffic lights at the bottom of the hill, then turn immediately right signposted Quays, and immediately left into Teign Street. Thomas Luny House is on your right.

THOMAS LUNY HOUSE
Owners: Alison and John Allan
Teign Street
Teignmouth
Devon TQ14 8EG
tel: (01626) 772976
4 rooms with private bathrooms
From £30 per person
Closed mid-December to February
Children over 12
Wolsey Lodge

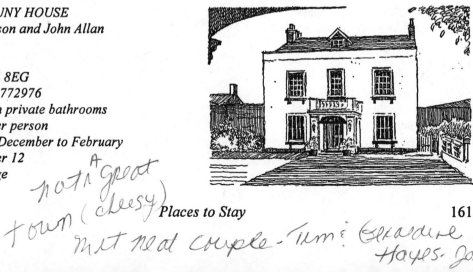

not a great town (cheesy)
met neal couple - Tim & Geraldine Hayes-Jones

When I saw Brattle House, clad with weatherboard and mellow Kent peg tile, it looked like an ordinary home, so I was thrilled to enter the wide, pine front door and discover that the house dates back to the 1600s. The cozy, oak-beamed sitting room opens up to a conservatory where afternoon tea and breakfast are served. Glasses and ice are provided so that guests can bring their own alcohol to enjoy drinks before, during, and after dinner eaten by candlelight round an antique mahogany table. Mo and Alan Rawlinson join guests, after the first course, for convivial evenings of dining and conversation. Up the wide staircase, two spacious front bedrooms enjoy broad window seats overlooking the fields to the distant church tower, but I must admit that my heart was won by the cozy little back bedroom with its idyllic view across the garden to open countryside. The Rawlinsons' most popular (fine-weather) excursion (apart from nearby Sissinghurst Castle and gardens) involves taking the old Kent and West Sussex steam train from Tenterden (past the house) to Northiam, then a little wooden ferry to Bodiam Castle, where you enjoy tea at Knollys before touring the castle and reversing your journey to Tenterden. *Directions:* From Tenterden, take the A28 towards Hastings for a short distance, proceeding down the hill and turning right towards Cranbrook. Brattle House is on the left after ¼ mile.

BRATTLE HOUSE   **NEW**
Owners: Mo and Alan Rawlinson
Watermill Bridges
Tenterden
Kent TN30 6UL
tel: (01580) 763565
3 rooms with private bathrooms
From £26 per person
Closed Christmas and New Year
Children over 15
Wolsey Lodge

It is said that Admiral Lord Nelson and the Duke of Wellington were once guests at Littleburn and the conviviality of those long-ago house-parties is still echoed today in Diana and Donald Cameron's soirees. They have lived all over the world and have always enjoyed entertaining and welcoming visitors: the only difference nowadays is that guests are paying bed-and-breakfast patrons. Early arrivals are welcomed with tea, shown to their rooms and invited to join Donald and Diana for pre-dinner drinks in the drawing room which, paneled in old pine and overlooking green fields and hills across the lawn, is a particularly attractive room. In the dining room the elegant table is laid with Waterford crystal and silver service. After dinner, guests are settled in the drawing room to be joined for conversation and drinks by their hosts and the friendly King Charles spaniels, Sophie and Poppy, who affectionately vie for visitors' attentions. On chilly evenings an open log fire adds cheer to the occasion. There are many spots to visit including Aysgarth Falls, Malham Tarn, Hardraw Falls, Jervaulx Abbey, Fountains Abbey, and Newby Hall and gardens. *Directions:* Turn south to Thoralby from the A684 just east of Aysgarth village. Upon entering Thoralby, turn right at the post office/shop onto a minor road. Pass the George Inn on the right and bear left at the next fork for Littleburn: the house is on the right just after the little bridge.

LITTLEBURN
Owners: Diana and Donald Cameron
Thoralby
Leyburn
Yorkshire DL8 3BE
tel: (01969) 663621
3 rooms with private bathrooms
From £29 per person
Closed Christmas
Children not accepted
Wolsey Lodge

The quiet village of Thornton Rust is in the heart of the Yorkshire Dales and Thornton Rust Hall nestles below green rocky fields within a sheltered, flower-filled garden. The Hall, dating from 1667 and 1702, underwent a complete and careful restoration just before the Coopers moved in. (Gillian and Alan added an indoor, heated swimming pool and a hard tennis court.) Upstairs, two large sunny bedrooms have their bathrooms ensuite while two additional bedrooms share a bathroom. Gillian ensures that guests are well looked after and well fed. Guests dine together round the dining room table and a typical main course might be a traditional roast beef accompanied by vegetables fresh from the garden. After dinner guests can enjoy a game of billiards in the enormous billiard-room or retire to the cozy sitting room to enjoy homemade brandy snaps and coffee. With a lifetime spent in the Yorkshire Dales, Gillian and Alan are happy to assist in planning walking and driving tours that encompass the stunning scenery and visit the market towns made famous by the Herriot television series. The ancient castles at Bolton, Skipton, and Middleham and the old abbeys of Jervaulx, Fountains, and Bolton are also worth a visit. The Hall also has three self-catering cottages available for weekly rentals. *Directions:* Leave the A1 at Leeming Bar and take the A684 via Bedale and Leyburn to Aysgarth where there is a left turn for Thornton Rust.

THORNTON RUST HALL
Owners: Gillian and Alan Cooper
Thornton Rust
Leyburn
Yorkshire DL8 3AW
tel: (01969) 663569
4 rooms, 2 with ensuite bathrooms
From £32 per person
Closed Christmas
Children over 8

Thornton Watlass is a delightful Wharfedale village set amongst gently rolling farmland where quiet, narrow lanes lead you to the heart of the magnificent Yorkshire Dales. How fortunate that this lovely spot offers an award-winning bed and breakfast The Old Rectory, a substantial Georgian home decked with wisteria, roses, and jasmine just at the edge of the village green. Olivia and Richard Farnell are justifiably proud that they won the prestigious English Tourist Board "England for Excellence" award in 1992. Olivia is the talented seamstress and decorator responsible for the enviable decor of softly hued sponged walls complementing the beautiful fabrics. The premier bedroom has a spectacular, softly draped half-tester bed and ensuite bathroom. The blue double room and spacious twin, decorated in pale shades of yellow and green, share a large bathroom and a smaller shower room ensuring that guests always have private facilities. Guests have their own immaculate sitting room where a log fire burns in the winter and they can enjoy tea and crumpets. Breakfast is the only meal served and Olivia and Richard spoil you for choice with their suggestions of restaurants and pubs. Arm yourself with one of the Farnell's driving routes that guide you through the Yorkshire Dales. *Directions:* From Bedale take the B6268 towards Masham and Thornton Watlass is signposted to your right down 2½ miles of narrow country lanes.

THE OLD RECTORY
Owners: Olivia and Richard Farnell
Thornton Watlass
Nr Masham
Yorkshire HG4 4AH
tel: (01677) 423456
3 rooms with private bathrooms
2 night minimum
From £30 per person
Open all year
Children over 12

The huge stone cheese presses in the McGinns' paddock mark the border between England and Wales, making this an ideal base for your explorations of North Wales and for visits to the walled Roman town of Chester. Valerie and John McGinn have done the most incredible job of converting what was previously a Georgian stable block into a lovely home. Guest accommodation is offered in three delightful ground floor rooms each accompanied by a sparkling ensuite bathroom. Two bedrooms open up to private patios, while a third offers wheelchair access from the cobbled courtyard. In warmer weather, guests breakfast in the spacious conservatory whose windows open to views of the large fishpond and pretty countryside views across the ha-ha. Guests are welcome to use the sheltered tennis court or enjoy croquet on the lawn. South Cheshire is renowned for cheese making and you can visit local producers and watch cheese being made by traditional methods. *Directions:* From Chester, take the A41 towards Whitchurch. At the pub New Inn, turn right onto B5069 to Malpas and turn left and then the first right at The Crown pub towards Wrexham. After 3 miles, pass a small filling station and the red-brick wall which borders Broughton House which is on your left before you reach the signpost for Clywd.

BROUGHTON HOUSE **NEW**
Owners: Valerie and John McGinn
Threapwood
Malpas
Cheshire SY14 7AN
tel and fax: (01948) 770610
3 rooms with private bathrooms
From £27 per person
Closed Christmas
Children over 10
No Smoking house

From a country road just off the A1 (London to Scotland road), you sweep down a gravel driveway to Tickencote Hall, a grand, mellow-stone manor surrounded by acres of parkland backing onto the tiny village of Tickencote with its quaint stone cottages. Dating from 1705, Tickencote Hall is home to Peter and Tarn Dearden and their three grown sons. I found the drawing room and dining room to be the height of country-house elegance, but was disappointed that the one bedroom I was able to see was, in comparison, drearily decorated. The Hall is run on traditional Wolsey Lodge house-party lines, where guests gather for drinks in the drawing room before dining together. Nearby Stamford, with its fine Georgian buildings and narrow alleyways full of interesting antique shops, pubs, and restaurants is a "must visit." In summer there's open-air Shakespearean theater at nearby Tolethorpe. Tarn is happy to supply a picnic for this, or provide two courses of dinner before the performance and two courses on your return. *Directions:* Take the A1 north to the Stamford roundabout, continue north on the A1 for 4 miles passing two left turns and the Tickencote sign, and turn left into the Texaco garage. Cross the forecourt and turn right towards Tickencote, ignoring the "Village Only" sign. Tickencote Hall's drive is on your left after 15 yards, opposite a wooden bus shelter.

TICKENCOTE HALL　　　**NEW**
Owners: Tarn and Peter Dearden
Tickencote
Stamford
Lincolnshire PE9 4AE
tel and fax: (01780) 65155
4 rooms, 2 with private bathrooms
From £35 per person
Closed Christmas
Credit cards: EC, MC, VS
Children over 12
Wolsey Lodge

Claiming the honor of being King Arthur's legendary birthplace, the ruins of Tintagel Castle cling to a wild headland exposed to the coastal winds. It's a place of myths that attracts visitors who come to soak up its fanciful past and enjoy its rugged scenery. While the village of Tintagel is a touristy spot, just a mile away lies the quiet hamlet of Trenale, a cluster of cottages, and the delightful Trebrea Lodge. Behind the impressive, tall Georgian facade lies a much older building of cozy, comfortable rooms. Upstairs the drawing room is full of splendid antiques but you will probably find yourself downstairs toasting your toes by the fire enveloped by a large armchair, enjoying drinks and coffee after a delicious dinner in the paneled dining room with its views across stone-walled fields to the distant sea. We particularly enjoyed our room (4) furnished, as are all the rooms, with lovely antiques and enjoying a large bathroom, the four-poster room (1) with its ornately carved Victorian four-poster bed, and room 5 a delightful twin bedded room with its view to the distant ocean. A tempting array of hot breakfast dishes is placed on the buffet for guests to help themselves. Walkers enjoy spectacular clifftop walks along rugged headlands. To the north lies Clovelly. *Directions:* From Tintagel take the road towards Boscastle. At the edge of the village turn right at the church (contemporary). Turn right at the top of the lane and Trebrea Lodge is on your left.

TREBREA LODGE
Owners: John Charlick and Sean Devlin
Trenale, Tintagel
Cornwall PL34 0HR
tel: (01840) 770410
8 bedrooms with private bathrooms
From £29 per person
Open all year
Children over 5
Smoking in 1 public room

Marjorie and Euan Aitken's home is a picture-book, thatched cottage in an idyllically quiet Oxfordshire village, nestled beside a duck pond with a row boat moored beneath overhanging willows. When the Aitkens restored the cottage they preserved all the lovely old features they uncovered: an old range and copper boiler, beams with the carpenter's identification marks, and a pump. Every room is furnished with antiques and decorated with collections of bric-a-brac and country bygones. Across the green-lawned farmyard the timbered barn has been converted to provide six immaculate guestrooms with modern showers, televisions, exposed beams, and displays of Marjorie's collections. I particularly enjoyed Mary (the rooms are named after royals), its corridor hung with farm implements, a Cumberland quilt decorating the bedroom wall, and its choirboy vestments cupboard used as a closet. Breakfast is the only meal served in the country pine breakfast room. Guests sometimes practice their golf swing (clubs provided) in the adjacent field where the grass is kept mowed by Hercules the plump, pet ram. Oxford Colleges, less than half an hour away, are a popular sightseeing spot, as is Blenheim Palace. Waddesden Manor, the ancestral Rothschild home, has a spectacular art collection. *Directions:* Exit the M40 at junction 6 and take the B4009 to Chinnor where you turn left on the B4445 towards Thame. After 2 miles turn right to Towersey, right at the cross roads, and the farm is on your left at the end of the village.

UPPER GREEN FARM
Owners: Marjorie and Euan Aitken
Manor Road
Towersey
Oxon OX9 3QR
tel: (01844) 212496 fax: (01844)260399
8 rooms with private bathrooms
From £19 per person
Open all year
Children over 13

Pat and Richard Mason transformed a tumbledown cottage and barn in an overgrown field by a stream into a delightful home facing a pretty lake with an idyllic garden full of unusual plants. Inside, the house is just as attractive as out. Sofas are drawn up around the wood-burning stove in the beamed sitting room. Upstairs, the two bedrooms are adjacent to each other and a shower room (a super-large cubicle with steam as well as shower). The three rooms handily make into a family suite. When there are two parties of guests, the large double room has the private use of the shower room while the small blue twin has the private use of an additional bathroom down the hall. Breakfast is the only meal served: guests sometimes walk to the local pub for dinner, but more often than not they drive to the Mayfly pub which offers good food and a pretty view of the River Test. One of Pat's suggested day trips is to visit the national rose collection at Mottisfont Abbey, Hilliers Arboretum, and Broadlands, the former home of Lord Mountbatten. Salisbury and Winchester are 15 miles distant. *Directions:* From the A303, at Andover, take the A3057 (Stockbridge road) and turn first right, signposted for Upper Clatford. Take the first left, go right at the T junction, and turn right opposite the Crook and Shears pub into a little lane which leads to Malt Cottage.

MALT COTTAGE   **NEW**
Owners: Pat and Richard Mason
Upper Clatford
Andover
Hampshire SP11 7QL
tel: (01264) 323469 fax: (01264) 334100
2 rooms with private bathrooms
From £18 per person
Closed Christmas
Children welcome

Upton House, a 12th-century village manor house, offers guests a winning combination: a lovely house with country-cottage coziness, outstanding decor, treasured antiques, carefully tended, flower-filled gardens, and a charming hostess. In the sitting room plump sofas covered in soft pink or blue brocade are grouped before the fireplace. In the adjacent dining room soft primrose walls highlight the ancient beams and a log fire blazes in the fireplace whose ornate pine mantle is decked with delicate china. From the dining room a private staircase leads to the Pink Bedroom, a twin-bedded room where everything from the tiny flowered bag containing guest soap to the pretty floral curtains coordinates with the muted pink walls. Up the main cottage staircase are two equally lovely rooms. Angela has paid attention to the smallest details: tea caddies are packed with every imaginable type of tea, fine china graces the tea trays, and the bathrooms are supplied with every extra. Five hot courses are always available for dinner if reservations are made in advance. There are enough activities nearby to occupy a week and the Jeffersons have maps marked for exploration of the Elgar Trail, the Potteries, Shakespeare country, and the Cotswolds. *Directions:* Upton Snodsbury is located 6 miles east of Worcester on the A422. Turn right by the Red Lion on the B4082 towards Pershore and Upton House is by the church.

UPTON HOUSE
Owners: Angela and Hugh Jefferson
Upton Snodsbury
Worcester
Worcestershire WR7 4NR
tel: (01905) 381226
3 rooms with private bathrooms
From £32.50 per person
Closed Christmas
Children not accepted
Wolsey Lodge

On every research trip we find a very special place to stay and in 1992 it was Beryl, a Gothic revival mansion on 13 acres of grounds. Special not only because of its location, just a mile from Wells cathedral or because it is a beautifully decorated home full of lovely antiques, but because of the special way that Holly and Eddie give of themselves to their guests. The measure of their success is the number of returning guests who bring their family, friends, and even dogs (provided that they are compatible with the resident chocolate labs). Lovers of elegant antiques will delight in every nook and cranny of Beryl—Eddie is a well-known antique dealer. All the bedrooms have special features. We loved our room, Summer, all pretty in pink and white with daisies on the wallpaper and bedcovers. Next door, Spring has an elegantly draped, four-poster bed to leap (literally) into. Choose Winston if you have a passion for grand, old-fashioned, climb-into bathtubs; Butterfly if you enjoy space and want to wake up with Wells cathedral framed in the enormous bay window. Wells is England's smallest city, with the most glorious cathedral. *Directions:* Leave or approach Wells on the B3139 in the direction of Radstock. Turn into Hawkers Lane (not Beryl Lane) opposite the Texaco garage. Drive to the top of the lane and continue straight into Beryl's driveway.

BERYL
Owners: Holly and Eddie Nowell
Hawkers Lane
Wells
Somerset BA5 3JP
tel: (01749) 678738 fax: (01749) 670508
7 bedrooms with private bathrooms
From £30 per person
Open all year
Credit cards: EC, MC, VS
Children welcome
Wolsey Lodge

Built in 1280 by monks from the Wilmington Priory, this parsonage is reputedly the oldest small medieval house still inhabited in England. The outside walls are of flint with green stone dressing, while the inside are constructed of blocks of chalk supporting huge oak beams and are studded with little leaded windows and narrow, wooden doors. On chilly mornings, guests enjoy breakfast at little tables set before a blazing log fire in the baronial sitting room. A narrow, stone staircase winds up from here to the Hall, where a four-poster bed sits beneath a high, timbered ceiling. The Solar is also accessed by way of a narrow spiral staircase. Here the bed sits beneath a beautiful wooden ceiling and little windows that open to views of the adjacent churchyard. All the bath/shower rooms are in a part of the house that was added in Victorian times, so guests have to pad the halls to reach 20th-century facilities. A popular day hike takes you through the surrounding forest to East Dean, along the famous Seven Sisters chalk cliffs, and back to West Dean. Glynebourne is a 20-minute drive away. *Directions:* From Brighton, take the A27 (Eastbourne road) past Lewes and after a 20-minute drive turn right towards Alfriston, left to Litleton, right at the T junction towards East Dean, and left following the narrow, one-way road through the hamlet to The Old Parsonage beside the church.

THE OLD PARSONAGE   **NEW**
Owners: Angela and Raymond Woodhams
West Dean
Alfriston, nr Seaford
East Sussex BN25 4AL
tel: (01323) 870432
3 rooms with private bathrooms
From £25 per person
Closed Christmas and New Year
Children over 12
No Smoking house

The Citadel sits like a mighty fortress on a knoll overlooking verdant countryside. As soon as you cross the threshold you realize this is not a "castle" of drafty halls and stone chambers but a lovely home built to a fanciful design. A spacious sitting room occupies one of the turrets and leads to the large billiard room. Sylvia and her husband, Beverly, often join guests for sherry before dinner and then guests dine together round the long dining-room table. You are welcome to bring your own wine. Up the broad staircase, two of the bedrooms occupy turrets. I particularly enjoyed the one at the front of the house with its adjacent, Victorian-style bathroom with center-stage clawfoot tub. A small twin-bedded room has an ensuite shower room. The adjacent golf club is a popular venue, but the real magic of the area lies in a visit to Hawkstone Park where you follow an intricate network of pathways through woodlands and across a narrow, log bridge to high cliffs, a ruined castle, mystical grotto, and giant obelisk. The Ironbridge Gorge Museums, Shrewsbury and Chester are within an hour's drive. *Directions:* From Shrewsbury, take the A49 (north) for 12 miles, turn right for Hodnet and Weston-under-Redcastle, and The Citadel is on your right, ¼ mile after leaving Weston-under-Redcastle (before Hawkstone Park).

THE CITADEL **NEW**
Owner: Sylvia and Beverly Griffiths
Weston-under-Redcastle
Shrewsbury
Shropshire SY4 5JY
tel: (01630) 685204
3 rooms with private bathrooms
From £30 per person
Open mid-March to November
Credit cards: EC, MC, VS
Children over 12
No Smoking house
Wolsey Lodge

Willersey's duck pond sits on the village green overlooked by golden-stone cottages. The little lane that runs beside the pub leads to The Old Rectory, sitting in a spacious garden with the 11th century village church as its closest neighbor. Another neighbor is a friendly farmer (an ex-jockey who rode for the Queen Mother) who welcomes guests who come to see his lambs in the spring. Bedrooms in The Old Rectory come in all shapes and sizes, from a snug attic room where bathrobes are provided for padding across the hall to grander ensuite rooms with four-poster beds. If you want complete privacy, opt for either the Bridle or Saddle rooms found in the converted stables overlooking the lovely garden. Bedrooms have everything from satellite television to quality toiletries. Individual tables are set for breakfast. In the evening guests usually stroll down to the Bell for dinner, flashlights are provided for guiding your way home. The Old Rectory is a perfect base for touring the pretty Cotswold villages and visiting manor houses and gardens. A delightful daytrip takes you farther afield to Stratford-upon-Avon and Warwick Castle. *Directions:* From Broadway, take the B4632 (Stratford-upon-Avon) for 1½ miles to Willersey. Turn right into Church Street at the Bell, and The Old Rectory is at the end of the lane.

THE OLD RECTORY   **NEW**
Owners: Liz and Chris Beauvoisin
Willersey
Broadway
Worcestershire WR12 7PN
tel and fax: (01386) 853729
8 rooms with private bathrooms
From £30 per person
Closed Christmas
Credit cards: EC, MC, VS
Children over 8
No Smoking house

Stratford-upon-Avon is a Mecca for visitors who come for everything associated with Shakespeare: the performances of his plays, the town's Tudor buildings, Anne Hathaway's cottage, and Mary Arden's house. Just across the garden from Mary Arden's house you find Pear Tree Cottage, home to Margaret and Ted Mander for almost forty years. A home which has been sympathetically extended to provide seven ensuite bedrooms for guests. All the rooms are delightful, though I particularly enjoyed those in the old cottage simply because they have an especially old-world feeling. Guests have an attractive little sitting room and breakfast room with little tables and chairs set in front of a dresser displaying decorative blue and white plates. Two modern kitchens are available for guests to prepare their picnics or suppers. Across the lane a pair of delightful little cottages are available on a weekly letting basis. Margaret and Ted supply guests with a map that outlines the vast array of places to visit in the area. *Directions:* From Stratford-upon-Avon, take the A3400 signposted for Henley-in-Arden for 2½ miles. Turn left to Wilmcote and Pear Tree Cottage is in the center of the village.

PEAR TREE COTTAGE   **NEW**
Owners: Margaret and Ted Mander
Church Road
Wilmcote
Stratford-upon-Avon
Warwickshire CV37 9UX
tel: (01789) 205889 fax: (01789) 262862
7 rooms with private bathrooms
From £20 per person
Closed Christmas
Children over 2

Vic builds houses for a living so when he came to remodel a small cottage into his family home, he put a priority on craftsmanship building the house in a traditional Cotswold style with spacious rooms and an enormous billiard room at the heart of the house. Beyond the billiard room guests enjoy a large sitting room with feather-pillowed sofas and French windows opening up to views of rolling farmland. Up the broad staircase are three guest bedrooms. A four-poster room and a small twin-bedded room share a bathroom while the principal bedroom enjoys a four-poster bed and a large ensuite bathroom with corner tub. Breakfast is the only meal served. If guests want to splurge, Angela recommends the Wesley in Winchcombe. Winchcombe is a very attractive village of mellow stone houses and shops stretched along the main road. The castle in the village (Sudeley Castle) is more of a stately home than a traditional castle. Exploring Cotswold villages is a popular pastime, with Bourton-on-the-Water, Stow-on-the-Wold, Chipping Campden, and Broadway being popular destinations. Navigate the quiet lanes to Upper and Lower Slaughter, Upper and Lower Swell, and Snowshill to see a more peaceful side of the Cotswolds. *Directions:* From Oxford take the A34 towards Stratford-upon-Avon to the A44 to Broadway where you turn left on the B4632 towards Cheltenham. One mile before reaching Winchcombe a large brown sign indicates a right turn to Winchcombe Potteries: turn left opposite this sign into Ireley Grounds' driveway.

IRELEY GROUNDS
Owners: Angela and Vic Sims
Broadway Road
Winchcombe
Gloucestershire GL54 5NY
tel: (01242) 603582 fax:(01242) 603443
3 rooms, 1 ensuite
From £20 per person
Open all year
Children over 7

Winchelsea is one of the earliest examples of town planning, having been rebuilt in 1277 after being devastated by the marauding French. The hilltop site is crowned by a church and surrounded by streets of enviable houses. Among the quiet byways are two pubs, a shop, a post office, and a tea shop (the Tea Tree). Set on a cliff, overlooking the marshes, Cleveland House provides a serene contrast to the bustle of nearby Rye and a base for your explorations of southern Sussex and Kent. The Jempsons' 18th-century home is fronted by over an acre of manicured lawns, appealing flower borders, a walled vegetable garden, and a sheltered heated swimming pool (May to September). The house is furnished with antiques and from the flagstone hallway guests have their private staircase which leads to two pretty bedrooms. As you lie in bed in the front bedroom you have exquisite views through floor-length windows towards the distant sea. The bathroom is a few steps down the hall. The pretty twin-bedded room has a small shower room ensuite. Both rooms have televisions and tea and coffee trays. Cliff, the gardener, is often on hand to discuss his vegetables and flowers and guests are encouraged to use the lovely swimming pool. Sitting rooms are reserved for family use. Breakfast is the only meal served. *Directions:* From Rye, take the A259 to Winchelsea (2 miles). Go up the hill, through the arch, take the first left and Cleveland House is the first home on the left.

CLEVELAND HOUSE   **NEW**
Owners: Sarah and Jonathan Jempson
Winchelsea
East Sussex TN36 4EE
tel: (01797) 226256 fax: (0179) 225080
2 rooms with private bathrooms
From £25 per person
Open all year
Credit cards: EC, MC, VS
Children welcome
No Smoking house

The Wykeham Arms is a very extraordinary Victorian pub: over 600 pictures decorate the walls, 1,000 tankards hang from beams, walls, and windows, and Winchester memorabilia abounds—many of the tables are old desks from nearby Winchester College. The menu, posted on the board in the bar, offers choices ranging from elaborate fare to tasty pub grub. Quieter tables can be reserved in the Bishop's Bar or the Watchmaker's Room with its pictures of an old-time watchmender. A family Bible sits atop a lectern outside the breakfast room. Up narrow stairways, the pretty bedrooms are not elaborate, but several have views across the chimney tops. Small refrigerators are stocked with very reasonably priced drinks. Because The Wykeham Arms is located in a pedestrian zone, all is peace and quiet (except on Friday morning when barrels of beer are rolled across the cobbles at 7:30 am). You can wander along the lovely old streets, stroll through the King's Gate and across the lawns to Winchester Cathedral with its seven chapels, medieval wall paintings, and royal tombs, and walk to everything in Winchester. *Directions:* Winchester is between junctions 9 and 10 on the M3. The Wykeman Arms is located near the cathedral. Graeme will send you a map which will enable you to navigate your car through the pedestrian zone to the pub's car park.

THE WYKEHAM ARMS
Owners: Anne and Graeme Jameson
75 Kingsgate Street
Winchester
Hampshire SO23 98T
tel: (01962) 853834   fax: (01962) 854411
7 rooms with private bathrooms
Double from £75.00
Open all year
Credit cards all major
Children over 14

In the Lake District it seems that run-of-the-mill hotels and guesthouses are a dime a dozen, so I was thrilled when I found an exceptional one in The Archway Guest House in the center of Windermere village. Hosts Aurea and Tony Greenhalgh serve mouthwatering breakfasts which offer homemade yogurt sweetened with a dash of honey and topped with fruit puree, freshly squeezed juices, American pancakes with syrup, and apple griddle cakes with butter and syrup as well as a traditional farmhouse breakfast. The Greenhalghs pride themselves on serving homemade foods, using organic ingredients whenever possible. Dinners are fresh and delicious and are accompanied by a choice of six red and six white wines. All the rooms are decorated in keeping with a Victorian home, from country pine in the dining room to antique quilts gracing the beds. Up the narrow, steep stairs the bedrooms and bathrooms are small, even tiny, but are very well equipped. The Archway is located in the heart of the Lake District, an area known for its outstanding beauty. An information book in every bedroom lists walks in the area for which Tony supplies maps. More leisurely exercise can be obtained by strolling into town. *Directions:* Exit the M6 at junction 36 and take the A591 around Kendal towards Ambleside. Shortly after passing Windermere's train station, turn left on Elleray Road and right into College Road. The Archway is on the left.

THE ARCHWAY GUEST HOUSE
Owners: Aurea and Tony Greenhalgh
13 College Road
Windermere
Cumbria LA23 1BY
tel: (015394) 45613
5 rooms with private bathrooms
From £21 per person
Open all year
Children over 10
No Smoking house

Hawksmoor Guest House appears no different from the many other guesthouses on these well-traveled Lake District roads until one enters, sees, and appreciates the apple-pie-order of Robert and Barbara Tyson's home. The decor is not fancy or pretentious, for this is not an expensive country-house hotel, but it is well maintained: Robert boasts, "If it's broken or damaged today, it will be fixed tomorrow." The dining room is delightfully set with pink tablecloths covered with delicate lace and laid with silver service. Barbara is happy for guests to eat in or out, always willing to provide a traditional English three-course dinner of an appetizer, roast with three vegetables, and a dessert such as apple pie and custard. Guests have a small comfortable lounge at their disposal. The bedrooms are smallish but each is decorated with pretty flowered wallpaper with matching curtains and bedspreads, and all have an ensuite bathroom. Robert is an expert on the Lake District and even manages to suggest a sight or two to the hurried traveler who is dashing through this lovely part of England and using it as a one-night stop on the road between London and Edinburgh. He has found that these rushed travelers often return for a stay of several days. Windermere is in the heart of the busy southern Lake District, easily accessible from the M6. *Directions:* Windermere is just off the A591 Ambleside to Kendal road. Drive along New Road and look for Hawksmoor on the right just after the clock tower.

HAWKSMOOR GUEST HOUSE
Owners: Barbara and Robert Tyson
Lake Road
Windermere
Cumbria LA23 2EQ
tel: (015394) 42110
10 rooms with private bathrooms
From £24 per person
Closed December
Children over 6

Just five miles from the Georgian splendors of Bath, Burghope Manor is the 13th-century home of Liz and John Denning. Much of the present house dates from Tudor times and Burghope has strong associations with Henry VIII's prelate Archbishop Cranmer. Liz is a vivacious person who loves meeting people from all walks of life and all over the world and enjoys sharing her lovely home with them. Guests are encouraged to make themselves at home in the large, pink drawing room, though they often prefer the cozier confines of the morning room. Upstairs, the three spacious, lovely bedrooms are each accompanied by an ensuite bathroom with bath and shower. For dinner, guests stroll into Winsley, a typical, old, country village, to dine at the Seven Stars Pub or Nightingales Restaurant. If you are planning on staying a week or longer consider renting the Dower House, a three-bedroom, four-bathroom home which occupies a corner of the garden. There are enough activities in Bath to occupy a week, though nearby Bradford on Avon should not be missed. *Directions:* From Bath, take the A36 towards Warminster for 5 miles and turn left on the B3108 signposted Winsley and Bradford on Avon. Follow the road up into the village and, immediately after passing the 30 mph signs, turn left into a small lane to Burghope Manor.

BURGHOPE MANOR **NEW**
Owners: Liz and John Denning
Winsley
Bradford on Avon
Wiltshire BA15 2LA
tel: (01225) 723557 fax: (01225) 723113
3 rooms with private bathrooms
From £35 per person
Closed Christmas
Credit cards: all major
Children over 10

The Dower House faces directly down the main street of the small village of Winster in the heart of the Peak District National Park. The front door of this Elizabethan manor opens to a stone-flag hallway and a spacious living room with comfortable seating grouped round the fireplace. A hearty breakfast is the only meal served in the dining room. For dinner, guests often enjoy straightforward pub food at either the Bowling Green or the Miners Standard in the village. Up the broad staircase are three spacious bedrooms decorated in soft pastels—two have their private bathrooms across the hall while a third has its snug shower room cleverly tucked into a large closet. Be sure to visit Winster's ancient Market House, the first property in Derbyshire to be purchased by the National Trust. Helen, a Blue Badge tourist guide for Derbyshire, is happy to share her wealth of information on the area, from cycling down the Tissington and High Peak trails to touring Chatsworth, home of the Duke and Duchess of Devonshire. *Directions:* From Matlock, take the A6 towards Bakewell for 2 miles and turn left onto the B5057 for the 4-mile drive to Winster. The Dower House faces you as you drive down Main Street.

THE DOWER HOUSE   **NEW**
Owners: Helen Bastin and Geoff Dalton
Main Street
Winster
Derbyshire DE4 2DH
tel: (01629) 650213 fax: (01629) 650894
3 rooms with private bathrooms
From £20 per person
Open March to October
Children over 10

The Old Wharf's idyllic setting provides an entrancing first impression. A lane leading off the main highway wends its way down to a delightful small building hugging the edge of a tiny canal. Nearby, cows graze peacefully in meadows which stretch as far as the eye can see. The enclosed front patio is ablaze with a riot of color: a blowzy cottage garden of colorful flowers, beautifully manicured yet artfully exuberant. The side of the house that opens onto the meandering stream is laced with climbing pink roses. The spell of the initial impression remains unbroken when you go inside. Moira and David have taken an old warehouse and converted it into their home, incorporating an outstanding small bed and breakfast. The decor throughout is fresh and airy and extremely pretty. Moira has managed to cleverly combine lovely pastel fabrics with natural wood-finish antiques to achieve a very pretty country look. Primrose has a small double-bedded bedroom and a snug sitting room with tall windows opening up to views of the river and fields. A continental breakfast is included in the tariff. Breakfast is the only meal served. Within easy reach are the towns of the Sussex coast, Petworth House, and Arundel Castle. *Directions:* From Billingshurst take the A272 towards Petworth, cross the canal and river, and The Old Wharf is 50 yards after the river on the left.

THE OLD WHARF
Owners: Moira and David Mitchell
Wisborough Green
Billingshurst
Sussex RH14 OJG
tel: (01403) 784096 fax: (01403) 783456
4 rooms with private baths
From £22.50 per person
Closed Christmas
Credit cards: all major
Children over 12
No Smoking house

18 St Paul's Square is one of several large Victorian terrace homes which border a grassy square down one of York's quiet side streets. From the outside, it looks just like many other houses in this up and coming neighborhood, but inside it is delightfully different, showcasing colorful country Victorian decor by Ann and Mike Beaufoy. A sunny yellow hallway rises from the entry, setting the cheerful mood felt throughout the house. In the sitting room sage-green, leafy wallpaper serves as a backdrop for an old country dresser displaying blue and white willow dishes and an old gray marble fireplace looking much as it must have done in Victorian times. The bedrooms are spacious and airy. I particularly admired the double room with warm pine furniture and a brass and iron bedstead covered with a patchwork bedspread. It is a ten-minute walk from St Paul's Square to the walls which surround the historic city center. For sightseeing, after you have exhausted the many possibilities in York, there are excursions to the North York Moors and the Dales and tours of stately homes (Castle Howard is a must) and ecclesiastical ruins (Rievaulx and Fountains Abbey). *Directions:* Leave the A64, York ring road, at the A1036 in the direction of York city center. Pass the racecourse and as the walls of York come into view turn left on Holgate Road (A59 Harrogate). After crossing the railway tracks look for a right turn to St Paul's Square.

18 ST PAUL'S SQUARE
Owners: Ann and Mike Beaufoy
18 St Paul's Square
York Y02 4BD
tel: (01904) 629884
3 rooms with private bathrooms
From £30 per person
Closed Christmas
Children welcome
Wolsey Lodge

Just a few yards from York's city walls, South Parade is a private, cobbled street adjacent to a very busy main road. Inside Number 4 is a world of quiet repose, where you are invited to partake of tea and hot buttered scones in the elegant drawing room. Bedrooms are all furnished to the highest standards: bathrooms are sparkling and have powerful showers, brass fittings, and are well equipped with many extras. All the rooms are decorated in soft pastels, one in soft blue-grays, another in shades of peach with matching bedspreads and drapes coordinating with the wall covering. On the top floor, a larger suite with a sitting area and writing desk gives guests lots of room for relaxation should they prefer the privacy of their room to the drawing room. With advance notice Anne is happy to provide a three-course candlelit supper, and meals are taken in the below-stairs room that was once the kitchen. Anne and Robin are mines of information on York and the surrounding countryside and they really put themselves out to steer visitors in the right direction. Guests often enjoy a bus tour of the Dales and Moors. *Directions:* Leave the A64 (which forms the southern part of the York Outer Ring Road) at the A1036, in the direction of York city center, following signs for the racecourse. Pass the racecourse, and as you see the Odeon Cinema on the left turn right into a narrow street (next to a car showroom) which is South Parade.

4 SOUTH PARADE
Owners: Anne and Robin McClure
4 South Parade
York YO2 2BA
tel and fax: (01904) 628229
3 rooms with private bathrooms
From £35 per person
Closed Christmas
Children not accepted
No Smoking house

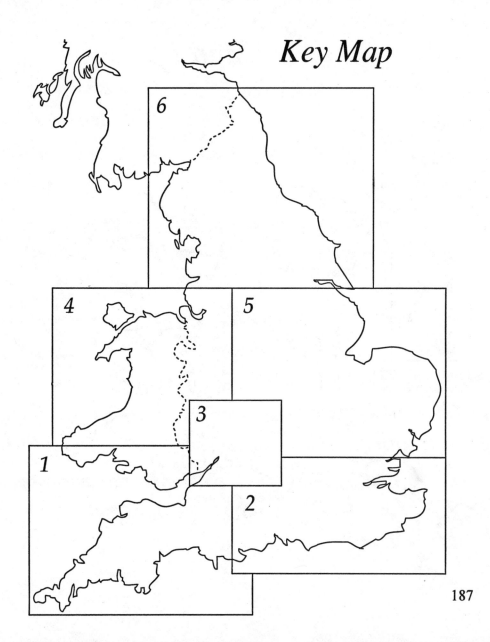

Key Map

6

4

5

3

1

2

187

Map 1

WALES

BRISTOL CHANNEL

ENGLISH CHANNEL

Willersey
Broadway
CHELTENHAM
Rendcomb
Oaksey
Ashton Keynes
St Briavels
Dursley
Grittleton
Calne
M50
M5
M4
M4
Nettleton
Bathford
BRISTOL
BATH
Bradford on Avon
Porlock
Wells
Winsley
Dunster
Glastonbury
Norton St Philip
Salisbury
Stogumber
Stoke St Gregory
Huish Champflower
Holford
Somerton
Rockbourne
Brithem Bottom
Curry Rivel
Parkham
Beercrocombe
Marnhull
East Coker
Honiton
Affpuddle
North Bovey
EXETER
Frampton
Tintagel
Crackington Haven
Chagford
Bovey Tracey
Dorchester
Manaton
Chudleigh
Haytor Vale
Teignmouth
Shaldon
Lanhydrock
Polperro
St Blazey
Harberton
PLYMOUTH
Dartmouth
Noss Mayo
Penzance
Golsithney
Penryn
Lizard
A39
A30
A30
A38
M4

● Places to Stay
○ Orientation / Sightseeing
✈ Airport

188

Map 2

ENGLISH
CHANNEL

- ● Places to Stay
- ○ Orientation
- ✈ Airport

189

Map 3

Places to Stay

Orientation

Airport

M5

A3400

A444

M6

M1

M40

Warwick

Hampton Lucy

Wilmcote

Loxley

Stratford upon Avon

A429

A41

Ettington

Hornton

Culworth

Upton Snodsbury

Banbury

Cropredy

Broad Campden

Chipping Campden

Shipston on Stour

Willersey

A3400

Broadway

Winchcombe

Evenlode

M50

Stow-on-the-Wold

Broadwell

A44

Woodstock

CHELTENHAM

Great Rissington

Rendcomb

A40

Burford

A429

Bourton-on-the-Water

A40

OXFORD

Lew

Northmoor

A40

Cirencester

Ampney Crucis

Dursley

Oaksey

A419

A433

Ashton Keynes

M4

A46

A429

Grittleton

M4

A419

M5

Nettleton

A419

190

Map 4

Isle of Anglesey

IRISH SEA

M6

M58

LIVERPOOL

M62

MANCHESTER

M53

CHESTER

Hargrave

STOKE ON TRENT

Threapwood

Llanymynech

Weston-under-Redcastle

M6

SHREWSBURY

WALES

Longnor

M54

● Places to Stay
○ Orientation/Sightseeing
✈ Airport

M5

Ludlow

WORCESTER

Upton Snodsbury

M50

Map 5

Langsett ●

Chinley ●

Holmesfield ●
Hathersage ●
Rowland ●

SHEFFIELD ○

Babworth ●

Lincoln ○

○ Bakewell

Leek ○
Bottomhouse ●
Blore ●

Winster ●
Tansley ●
Shottle ●
Ashbourne ○

NOTTINGHAM ○

Bourne ●

King's Lynn ○

Cley next the Sea ●

NORWICH ○
● Saxlingham Thorpe

Northwold ●

Long Stratton ●

LEICESTER ○
Hallaton ●
Tickencote ●

Stamford ○

Ely ●

Saxmundham ●

BIRMINGHAM ○
COVENTRY ○
Warwick ○
Stratford-upon-Avon ●

NORTHAMPTON ○

CAMBRIDGE ○

Otley ●

IPSWICH ○

Stoke by Nayland ●
Dedham ●
Higham ●
Bures ●
Colchester ○

NORTH SEA

Places to Stay ●
Orientation/Sightseeing ○
Airports ✈

OXFORD ○

Map 6

SCOTLAND

NORTH SEA

● Places to Stay
○ Orientation/Sightseeing
✈ Airports

○ CARLISLE

Boltongale ●

Corbridge ●

Hexham ●

✈ ○ NEWCASTLE UPON TYNE

Mungrisdale ●

Brandlingill ●
Brackenthwaite ●

○ Penrith

Rosthwaite ●

Ambleside ●

Little Langdale ●

Windermere ●

Blawith ●

Near Sawrey ●

Richmond ●

Dunsley ●   ○ Whitby

Reeth ●

Thornton Watlass ●

Hutton le Hole ●

Thornton Rust ●

Buckden ●

Thoralby ●

○ Scarborough

Kirkby Lonsdale ●

Austwick ●

Starbotton ●

Ramsgill ●

Crayke ●

Helperby ●

Bridlington ○

Capernwray ●

○ Harrogate

YORK ●

✈ ○ LEEDS

M621

M62

M62

M58

M6

M1

A1

A1

IRISH SEA

193

Places That Welcome Children

(no age limit)

Ashton Keynes, Cove House
Babworth, The Barns
Bath, Haydon House
Bath, Holly Lodge
Boldre, Boldre Hill
Bosham, Hatpins
Bottomhouse, Pethills Bank Cottage
Bourne, Bourne Eau House
Broad Campden, The Malt House
Broadway, Milestone House
Buckden, The Buck Inn
Burford, The Lamb Inn
Chiddingfold, Greenaway
Corbridge, Low Barns
Dartmouth, Ford House
Dunsley, Dunsley Hall
Dursley–Stinchcombe, Drakestone House
East Coker–Holywell, Holywell House
Frant, The Old Parsonage
Great Rissington, The Lamb Inn
Goldsithney, Ennys Farm
Hargrave, Greenlooms Cottage
Haytor Vale, The Rock Inn
Helperby, Brafferton Hall
Hexham, East Peterel Field Farm
Higham, The Old Vicarage

Holford, Quantock House
Hornton, The Manor House
Hutton le Hole, Hammer and Hand
Little Langdale, Three Shires Inn
Llanmynech, Vyrnwy Bank
Loxley, Loxley Farm
Mungrisdale, The Mill Hotel
Nettleton, Fosse Farmhouse
Norton St Philip, The Plaine Guest House
Ramsgill, The Yorke Arms
Reeth, The Burgoyne Hotel
Rowland, Holly Cottage
Rye, Jeake's House
Saxmundham–Hinton, High Poplars
Shipston on Stour, Longdon Manor
Shottle, Dannah Farm
Somerton, The Lynch Country House
St Briavels, Cinderhill House
Starbotton, Hilltop Country Guest House
Tansley, Lane End House
Threapwood, Broughton House
Upper Clatford, Malt Cottage
Wells, Beryl
Winchelsea, Cleveland House
York, 18 St Paul's Square

No Smoking Houses

Ampney Crucis, Waterton Garden Cottage

Bath, Haydon House

Bath, Holly Lodge

Bath, Somerset House

Boltongate, The Old Rectory

Bosham, Hatpins

Brackenthwaite, Pickett Howe

Bovey Tracey, Willmead Farm

Brandlingill, Low Hall

Brithem Bottom, Lower Beers

Broad Campden, Orchard Hill House

Cropredy, The Old Manor

Dunster, Dollons House

Dursley–Stinchcombe, Drakestone House

Ettington, Ettington Manor

Frittenden, Maplehurst Mill

Golden Green, Goldhill Mill

Hadlow, Leavers Oast

Hartfield, Bolebroke Mill

Headcorn, Vine Farm

Henley on Thames, Hernes

Holford, Quantock House

Horsted Keynes, Rixons

Langsett, Aldermans Head Manor

Lanhydrock, Treffry Farmhouse

Lizard, Landewednack House

Ludlow, Number Eleven

Maidenhead, Beehive Manor

Marnhull, Old Lamb House

Norton St Philip, The Plaine Guest House

Northmoor, Rectory Farm

Noss Mayo–Bridgend, Rowan Cottage

Oaksey, Oaksey Court

Parkham, The Old Rectory

Penshurst, Swale Cottage

Penryn, Clare House

Polperro–Pelynt, Trenderway Farm

Porlock, Bales Mead

Rogate, Mizzards Farm

Rosthwaite, Hazel Bank

Rye, Green Hedges

Salisbury, Stratford Lodge

Shipston on Stour, Longdon Manor

Speen, Speen Cottage

St Blazey, Nanscawen House

Stogumber, Curdon Mill

Tansley, Lane End House

West Dean, The Old Parsonage

Weston-under-Redcastle, The Citadel

Willersey, The Old Rectory

Windermere, The Archway Guest House

Wisborough Green, The Old Wharf

York, 4 South Parade

Members of Wolsey Lodges

Ashton Keynes, Cove House
Blore, The Old Rectory
Boltongate, The Old Rectory
Boldre, Boldre Hill
Bourne, Bourne Eau House
Bradford on Avon, Priory Steps
Brithem Bottom, Lower Beers
Calne, Chilvester Hill House
Capernwray, New Capernwray Farm
Chudleigh, Oakfield
Chinley, Ashen Clough
Cranbrook, The Old Cloth Hall
Culworth, Fulford House
Crayke, Halfway House
Dursley–Stinchcombe, Drakestone House
Ettington, Ettington Manor
Frittenden, Maplehurst Mill
Hallaton, The Old Rectory
Helperby, Brafferton Hall

Henley on Thames, Hernes
Higham, The Old Vicarage
Honiton, Woodhayes
Horsted Keynes, Rixons
Huish Champflower, Jews Farm House
Longnor, Moat House
Ludlow, The Lodge
Noss Mayo–Bridgend, Rowan Cottage
Oaksey, Oaksey Court
Saxmundham–Hinton, High Poplars
Teignmouth, Thomas Luny House
Tenterden, Brattle House
Thoralby, Littleburn
Tickencote, Tickencote Hall
Upton Snodsbury, Upton House
Wells, Beryl
Weston-under-Redcastle, The Citadel
York, 18 St Paul's Square

Index

A

Abbotts Ann
Abbotts Law, 16
About Bed And Breakfast Travel, 2
About England, 11
Affpuddle
The Old Vicarage, 17
Aldermans Head Manor, 101, 195
Alveston Cottage, 159
Ampney Crucis
Waterton Garden Cottage, 19, 195
Angel Inn, The, 156
Animals, 2
Appletree Holme Farm, 29
Archway Guest House, The, 180, 195
Arrival, 2
Ashen Clough, 53, 196
Ashton Keynes
Cove House, 20, 194, 196
Austwick
Wood View, 21

B

Babworth
The Barns, 22, 194

Bales Mead, 130, 195
Barns, The, 22, 194
Barracott, 113
Bath
Haydon House, 23, 194, 195
Holly Lodge, 24, 194, 195
Somerset House, 25, 195
Bathford
The Orchard, 26
Bathrooms, 2
Bedrooms, 3
Beehive Manor, 112, 195
Beercrocombe
Frog Street Farm, 27
Beryl, 172, 194, 196
Blawith
Appletree Holme Farm, 29
Blore
The Old Rectory, 30, 196
Boldre
Boldre Hill, 31, 194, 196
Bolebroke Mill, 85, 195
Boltongate
The Old Rectory, 32, 195, 196

C

I

J

K

L

Lamb Inn, Burford, 47, 194
Lamb Inn, Great Rissington, 78, 194
Landewednack House, 105, 195
Lane End House, 160, 194, 195
Langsett
    Aldermans Head Manor, 101, 195
Lanhydrock
    Treffry Farmhouse, 102, 195
Leavers Oast, 80, 195
Lew
    The Farmhouse Hotel and Restaurant, 103
Little Langdale
    Three Shires Inn, 104, 194
Little Orchard House, 142
Littleburn, 163, 196
Lizard
    Landewednack House, 105, 195
Llanmynech
    Vyrnwy Bank, 106, 194
Lodge, The, 111, 145, 196
Long Stratton
    Mayfield Farm, 107
Longdon Manor, 148, 194, 195
Longnor
    Moat House, 108, 196
Low Barns, 57, 194
Low Hall, 39, 195

Lower Beers, 40, 195, 196
Loxley
    Loxley Farm, 109, 194
Ludlow
    Number Eleven, 110, 195
    The Lodge, 111, 196
Lynch Country House, The, 150, 194

M

Maidenhead
    Beehive Manor, 112, 195
Malt Cottage, 170, 194
Malt House, The, 41, 194
Manaton
    Barracott, 113
Manor House, Hornton, 96, 194
Maplehurst Mill, 75, 195, 196
Maps, 5
Marnhull
    Old Lamb House, 114, 195
Mayfield Farm, 107
Meals, 5
Milestone House, 43, 194
Mill Hotel, The, 115, 194
Mizzards Farm, 137, 195
Moat House, Longnor, 108, 196
Mungrisdale
    The Mill Hotel, 115, 194

N

O

P

T

W

Y

We Love to Hear from Karen Brown's Readers

ACCOLADES: We'd love to hear which accommodations you have especially enjoyed—even the shortest of notes is greatly appreciated. It is reassuring to know that places we recommend meet with your approval.

COMPLAINTS: Please let us know when a place we recommend fails to live up to the standards you have come to expect from Karen Brown. Constructive criticism is greatly appreciated. We sometimes make a mistake, places change, or go downhill. Your letters influence us to re-evaluate a listing.

RECOMMENDATIONS: If you have a favorite hideaway that you would like to recommend, please write to us. Give us a feel for the place, if possible send us a brochure and photographs (which we regret we cannot return). Convince us that on our next research trip, your discovery deserves a visit. All accommodations included in our guides are ones we have seen and enjoyed. Many of our finest selections are those that readers have discovered—wonderful places we would never have found on our own.

Please send information to:

KAREN BROWN'S GUIDES
Post Office Box 70
San Mateo, California 94401, U.S.A.
Telephone (415) 342-9117   Fax (415) 342-9153

Be a Karen Brown's Preferred Reader

If you would like to be the first to know when new editions of Karen Brown's Guides go to press, and also to be included in any special promotions, simply send us your name and address. We encourage you to buy new editions and throw away the old ones. You'll be glad you did. Don't miss a wealth of wonderful new discoveries—or run the risk of staying in places that no longer meet our standards. We cover the miles searching for special places so that you don't have to spend your valuable vacation time doing so.

Name _____

Street _____

Town _____ State _____ Zip _____

Telephone: _____ Fax: _____

Please send information to:

KAREN BROWN'S GUIDES
Post Office Box 70
San Mateo, California 94401, U.S.A.
telephone (415) 342-9117   fax (415) 342-9153

Karen Brown's Country Inn Guides
The Most Reliable & Informative Series on Country Inns

Detailed itineraries guide you through the countryside. Every recommendation, from the most deluxe hotel to a simple B&B, is personally inspected, approved and chosen for its romantic ambiance and warmth of welcome. Our charming accommodations reflect every price range, from budget hideaways to the most luxurious palaces.

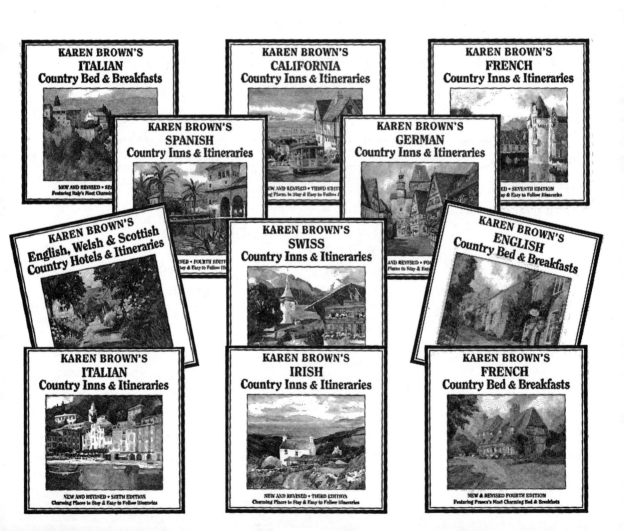

U.S.A. Order Form

Please ask in your local bookstore for KAREN BROWN'S GUIDES. If the books you want are unavailable, you may order directly from the publisher.

California Country Inns & Itineraries $14.95

English Country Bed & Breakfasts $15.95

English, Welsh & Scottish Country Hotels & Itineraries $14.95

French Country Bed & Breakfasts $15.95

French Country Inns & Itineraries $14.95

German Country Inns & Itineraries $14.95

Irish Country Inns & Itineraries $16.95

Italian Country Bed & Breakfasts $14.95

Italian Country Inns & Itineraries $16.95

Spanish Country Inns & Paradors $14.95

Swiss Country Inns & Itineraries $16.95

Name _____ Street _____

Town _____ State _____ Zip _____ tel. _____

Credit Card [MasterCard or Visa] _____ Exp: _____

Add $3.50 for the first book and .50 cents for each additional book for postage & packing. California residents add 8.25% sales tax. Order form only for shipments within the U.S.A. Indicate number of copies of each title; send form with check or credit card information to:

KAREN BROWN'S GUIDES
Post Office Box 70, San Mateo, California, 94401, U.S.A.
tel: (415) 342-9117   fax: (415) 342-9153

Karen Brown's
English, Welsh & Scottish Country Hotels
& Itineraries

The Choice of the Discriminating Traveler to Britain
Featuring Country House Hotels, Small London Hotels and Driving Itineraries

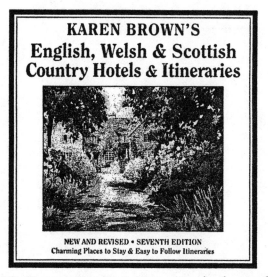

English Welsh & Scottish Country Hotels & Itineraries is the perfect companion guide to Karen Brown's *English Country Bed & Breakfast*s. The bed and breakfast guide features places to stay in private homes, pubs, and guesthouses. *English, Welsh & Scottish Country Hotels & Itineraries* features our personal selection of wonderful little hotels, a section on London hotels (in all price ranges), and detailed driving itineraries that cover Britain from John O'Groats to Lands End. Both books use the same maps, making it convenient to choose a combination of places to stay from each.

NOTES

NOTES

NOTES

NOTES

NOTES

KAREN BROWN wrote her first travel guide in 1979. Her personalized travel series has grown to eleven titles and Karen and her small staff work diligently to keep all the guides updated. Karen, her husband, Rick, and their children Alexandra and Richard, live on the coast south of San Francisco at their own country inn, Seal Cove Inn, in Moss Beach.

JUNE BROWN hails from Sheffield, England, has an extensive background in travel, dating back to her youth when she "youth hosteled" throughout Europe. June lives in San Mateo with her husband, Tony, and their children Simon and Clare.

BARBARA TAPP, the talented artist responsible for all the delightful illustrations in this guide, was raised in Australia where she studied interior design. Barbara works freelance as a pen and ink illustrator for real estate companies. She specializes in exteriors, interiors and gardens. Barbara lives in the San Francisco East Bay with her husband, Richard, and children Jonathan, Alexander and Georgia.

JANN POLLARD, the artist responsible for the cover painting, has studied art since childhood, and is well-known for her outstanding impressionistic-style water colors which she has exhibited in numerous juried shows, winning many awards. Jann travels frequently to Europe (using Karen Brown's guides) where she loves to paint. Jann lives in the Burlingame with her husband, Gene, and their two daughters.

SEAL COVE INN—LOCATED IN THE SAN FRANCISCO AREA

Karen Brown Herbert (best known as author of the Karen Brown's Guides) and her husband, Rick, have put seventeen years of experience into reality and opened their own superb hideaway, Seal Cove Inn. Spectacularly set amongst wild flowers and bordered by towering cypress trees, Seal Cove Inn looks out to the ocean over acres of county park: an oasis where you can enjoy secluded beaches, explore tide-pools, watch frolicking seals, and follow the tree-lined path that traces the windswept ocean bluffs. Country antiques, original-watercolors, flower-laden cradles, rich fabrics, and the gentle ticking of grandfather clocks create the perfect ambiance for a foggy day in front of a crackling log fire. Each bedroom is its own haven with a cozy sitting area before a wood-burning fireplace and doors opening onto a private balcony or patio with views to the distant ocean. Moss Beach is a 35-minute drive south of San Francisco, 6 miles north of the picturesque town of Half Moon Bay, and a few minutes from Princeton harbor with its colorful fishing boats and restaurants. Seal Cove Inn makes a perfect base for whale-watching, salmon-fishing excursions, day trips to San Francisco, exploring the coast, or best of all, just a romantic interlude by the sea, time to relax and be pampered. Karen and Rick look forward to the pleasure of welcoming you to their hideaway by the sea.

Seal Cove Inn, 221 Cypress Avenue, Moss Beach, California, 94038, U.S.A.
telephone: (415) 728-7325   fax: (415) 728-4116